CLASSIFYING LIVING THINGS

SCIENCE

MACMILLAN/McGRAW-HILL EDITION

CLASSIFYING LIVING THINGS

RICHARD MOYER ■ **LUCY DANIEL** ■ **JAY HACKETT**

PRENTICE BAPTISTE ■ **PAMELA STRYKER** ■ **JOANNE VASQUEZ**

NATIONAL
GEOGRAPHIC
SOCIETY

**McGraw-Hill
School Division**

New York   Farmington

PROGRAM AUTHORS

Dr. Lucy H. Daniel,
Teacher, Consultant
Rutherford County Schools,
North Carolina

Dr. Jay Hackett
Emeritus Professor of Earth
Sciences
University of Northern
Colorado

Dr. Richard H. Moyer
Professor of Science
Education
University of Michigan-
Dearborn

Dr. H. Prentice Baptiste
Professor of Curriculum and
Instruction
New Mexico State
University

Pamela Stryker, M.Ed.
Elementary Educator and
Science Consultant
Eanes Independent School
District
Austin, Texas

JoAnne Vasquez
Elementary Science
Education Specialist
Mesa Public Schools,
Arizona
NSTA President 1996–1997

NATIONAL
GEOGRAPHIC
SOCIETY

Washington, D.C.

CONTRIBUTING AUTHORS

Dr. Thomas Custer
Dr. James Flood
Dr. Diane Lapp
Doug Llewellyn
Dorothy Reid
Dr. Donald M. Silver

CONSULTANTS

Dr. Danny J. Ballard
Dr. Carol Baskin
Dr. Bonnie Buratti
Dr. Suellen Cabe
Dr. Shawn Carlson
Dr. Thomas A. Davies
Dr. Marie DiBerardino
Dr. R. E. Duhrkopf
Dr. Ed Geary
Dr. Susan C. Giarratano-Russell
Dr. Karen Kwitter
Dr. Donna Lloyd-Kolkin
Ericka Lochner, RN
Donna Harrell Lubcker
Dr. Dennis L. Nelson
Dr. Fred S. Sack
Dr. Martin VanDyke
Dr. E. Peter Volpe
Dr. Josephine Davis Wallace
Dr. Joe Yelderman

Invitation to Science, World of Science, and *FUNtastic Facts* features found in this textbook were designed and developed by the National Geographic Society's Education Division.

Copyright © 2000 National Geographic Society

The name "National Geographic Society" and the Yellow Border Rectangle are trademarks of the Society, and their use, without prior written permission, is strictly prohibited.

Cover Photo: *bkgd.* F.C. Millington/TCL Masterfile; *inset* John Lythgoe/TCL Masterfile.

McGraw-Hill School Division

A Division of The McGraw·Hill Companies

Copyright © 2000 McGraw-Hill School Division,
a Division of the Educational and Professional
Publishing Group of The McGraw-Hill Companies, Inc.

McGraw-Hill School Division
Two Penn Plaza
New York, New York 10121

Printed in the United States of America

ISBN 0-02-278215-X / 4

3 4 5 6 7 8 9 071/046 05 04 03 02 01 00

CONTENTS

REFERENCE SECTION

CLASSIFYING LIVING THINGS

CHAPTER 1

How LIVING THINGS ARE PUT TOGETHER

How can you tell something is a living thing? Do you see living things here? How can you tell? What do living things do that nonliving things don't do? What are living things made up of?

 In Chapter 1 look for and read lists. A list is a helpful way to put information together. You may have used a shopping list.

Topic
LIFE SCIENCE
1

WHY IT MATTERS

You can identify living and nonliving things by observing their characteristics.

SCIENCE WORDS

oxygen part of air; needed by most plants and animals to live

organism a living thing that carries out basic life functions on its own

cell the smallest unit of living matter

tissue a group of similar cells that work together to carry out a job

organ a group of tissues that work together to do a certain job

organ system a group of organs that work together to carry on life functions

Identifying Living Things

How do you know if something is living or not?

MEOW! A kitten runs by chasing a toy. The toy seems to try to escape from the kitten as it zips by. Both things seem to be similar. They both are made of parts. These parts work together to do jobs, like moving. However, they are not the same. One is living. One is nonliving. How can you tell?

EXPLORE

HYPOTHESIZE Sometimes it is hard to tell if an object is living or nonliving. However, living things have certain parts in common. What might they be? Write a hypothesis in your *Science Journal.*

Investigate What Living Things Are Made Of

Observe parts of an onion plant with a microscope and a hand lens.

MATERIALS

- onion plant
- prepared slides of onion skin and leaf
- hand lens
- microscope
- *Science Journal*

PROCEDURES

1. **OBSERVE** In your *Science Journal*, draw the whole onion plant. Label its parts. Write down how each part might help the plant live.

2. **OBSERVE** Ask your teacher to cut the plant lengthwise. Draw and label what you see.

3. **OBSERVE** Observe a small section of onion skin and a thin piece of a leaf with the hand lens. Draw what you see.

4. **OBSERVE** Use the microscope to look at the onion skin and the leaf section. Use high and low power. Draw what you see.

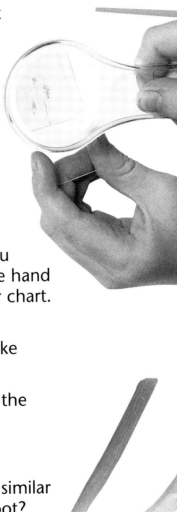

CONCLUDE AND APPLY

1. **COMMUNICATE** What did you see when you examined the onion skin and leaf with the hand lens and the microscope? Make a table or chart.

2. **COMPARE AND CONTRAST** How are your observations of the onion skin and leaf alike and different?

3. **DRAW CONCLUSIONS** What do the parts of the onion plant seem to be made of?

GOING FURTHER: Problem Solving

4. **EXPERIMENT** Do you think you would see similar structures if you observed a part of the root? How could you find out?

What Are Living Things?

Do you think you have anything in common with the onion plant shown in the Explore Activity? Although you aren't green and don't have leaves growing out the top of your head, you have more in common with an onion than you might imagine!

The one thing you have in common is that you are both living things. Most living things share certain characteristics. Among them are the basic needs for food, water, a place to live, and oxygen (ok′sə jən). Most living things use oxygen to turn food into energy. Plants need oxygen to use the food they make. Another characteristic of living things is that they are made of parts. Each part has a specific job to keep a living thing alive.

Plants, people, and other animals are all organisms (ôr′gə niz′əmz). An organism is a living thing that carries out five basic life functions on its own.

Organisms come in all shapes and sizes. Tiny flies, onion plants, great blue whales—even you—are all organisms. It doesn't matter if an organism lives in the water, on the ground, or in the tops of the tallest trees. All organisms carry out five basic life functions.

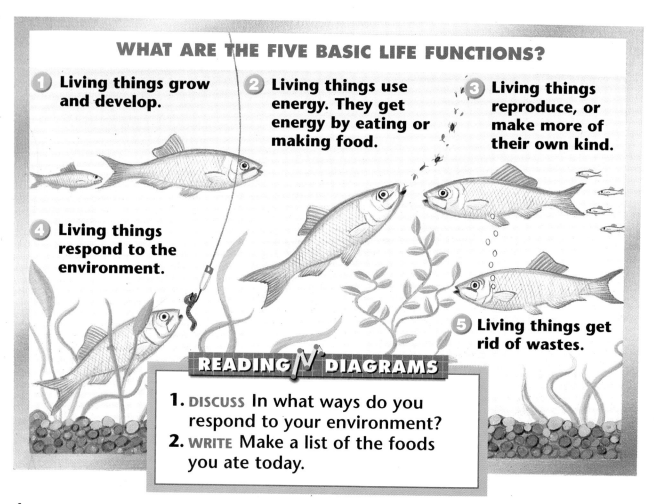

WHAT ARE THE FIVE BASIC LIFE FUNCTIONS?

1. Living things grow and develop.

2. Living things use energy. They get energy by eating or making food.

3. Living things reproduce, or make more of their own kind.

4. Living things respond to the environment.

5. Living things get rid of wastes.

READING DIAGRAMS

1. DISCUSS In what ways do you respond to your environment?
2. WRITE Make a list of the foods you ate today.

4

What Are Living Things Made Of?

The small, boxlike structures making up the onion plant in the Explore Activity are called **cells** (selz). A cell is the smallest unit of living matter. In other words cells are the "building blocks" of living things. All living things are made of cells—even you.

Although all living things are made of cells, all cells are not the same. The plant cells in the Explore Activity had a boxlike shape. Some even contained a green material, called *chlorophyll* (klôr′ə fil′). When sunlight strikes chlorophyll, the cell can make food for the plant. Animal cells don't contain chlorophyll and are not box shaped. You will learn more about plant and animal cells in Topic 2.

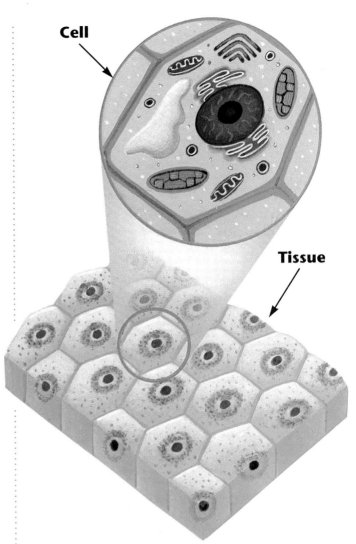

Cell

Tissue

Groups of cells form the tissues that make up an onion plant's leaves.

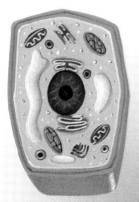

Plant cell

How are these two cells similar and different?

Animal cell

Cells Working Together

Cells are organized into **tissues** (tish′üz). A tissue is a group of similar cells that work together to carry out a job. In the onion plant, each layer of onion skin you observed is a tissue. Bones, muscles, and nerves are tissues in your body.

Each tissue has its own job, or function. In an onion plant, the tissues making up the roots absorb water. In your body, muscle and bone tissues work together to move you.

5

How Do Tissues Work Together?

Groups of tissues form organs (ôr'gənz). Organs are tissues that work together to do a certain job. Your brain and heart are two of the organs in your body. Your heart's job is to pump blood to all body tissues. What jobs does your brain do?

Roots, stems, and leaves are organs of an onion plant. A leaf is an organ that makes the food for the onion plant. What do the roots and stem do?

A group of parts that works together forms a *system*. An organ system (ôr'gən sis'təm) is a group of organs that work together to carry on life functions. A plant's roots, stem, and leaves are one organ system. In your body the digestive system is one example of an organ system. It breaks down food and absorbs the nutrients you need to live.

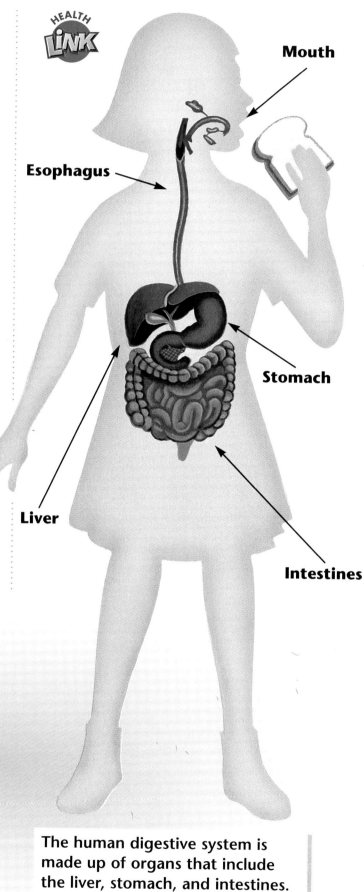

HEALTH LINK

Mouth

Esophagus

Stomach

Liver

Intestines

The human digestive system is made up of organs that include the liver, stomach, and intestines.

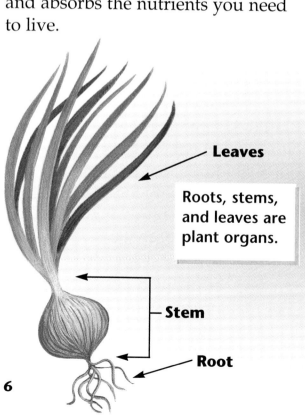

Leaves

Roots, stems, and leaves are plant organs.

Stem

Root

6

Are There One-Celled Organisms?

In this topic you learned that an organism is a living thing that carries out five basic life functions. To review, these basic life functions include:

- growing and developing
- using energy
- reproducing
- responding to the environment
- getting rid of wastes

An onion plant is made up of cells, tissues, organs, and organ systems. It uses these parts to carry out basic life functions.

Do you think that something that is made of only one cell and has no tissues, organs, or organ systems can be an organism? Why or why not?

Brain Power

Tell which of these is an organism. Explain why you think so. Hint: Which carries out all five basic life functions?

Putting It All Together

HYPOTHESIZE What body parts work together to allow you to perform a simple task like writing? Write a hypothesis in your *Science Journal.*

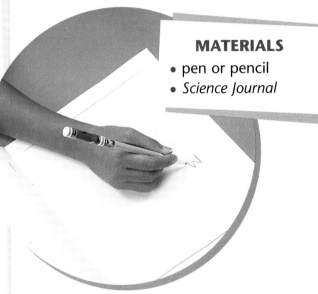

MATERIALS
- pen or pencil
- *Science Journal*

PROCEDURES

1. Write your name in your *Science Journal.*

2. **INFER** As you write think about what each body part, organ, and organ system is doing.

CONCLUDE AND APPLY

1. **COMMUNICATE** Write a paragraph that tells what organs you were using. Consider the organs you use to see, touch, breathe, and think.

2. **DRAW CONCLUSIONS** How did your body parts and organs work together to allow you to write?

What Kinds of Organisms Live in Pond Water?

Believe it or not, many different one-celled organisms live on Earth. You can even find many of them in a single drop of pond water.

What kinds of organisms are small enough to live in a drop of water? If you used a microscope to examine some pond water, you might see organisms like these.

Organisms that are so small you need a microscope to see them are called *microorganisms*.

Do any of these microorganisms have parts that might be helpful for living in water? What are they?

Many microorganisms are helpful. Many, like these, are a food source for other animals. Many feed on dead organisms in the water. Some can be harmful. They cause disease and illness in humans and other animals.

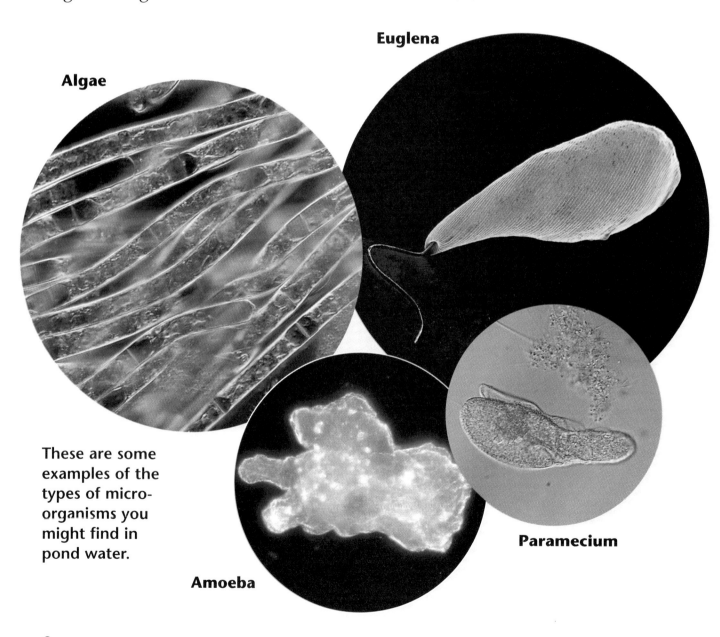

Euglena

Algae

Paramecium

Amoeba

These are some examples of the types of microorganisms you might find in pond water.

All living things have certain characteristics. Being able to recognize these characteristics lets you identify something as living or nonliving. Identifying something as a living thing helps you decide how to treat it. You would treat a doll very differently from a living baby!

A doll is not a living thing. What does a baby need that a doll does not?

REVIEW

1. How can you identify a living thing?

2. Name three living things. Explain how you know each is living. Be sure to include the five basic life functions.

3. What is an organ?

4. **COMMUNICATE** Give an example of an organ system. What does this system do?

5. **CRITICAL THINKING** *Apply* In what ways are microorganisms different from you? How are they similar to you?

WHY IT MATTERS THINK ABOUT IT A doll cries, moves its arms and legs, drinks a bottle, and wets a diaper. How do you know it is not an organism?

WHY IT MATTERS WRITE ABOUT IT What if your younger sister thinks her doll is a living thing? How would you explain to her that it is not a living thing?

READING SKILL Give an example of a list that you found in this topic. What was the list about?

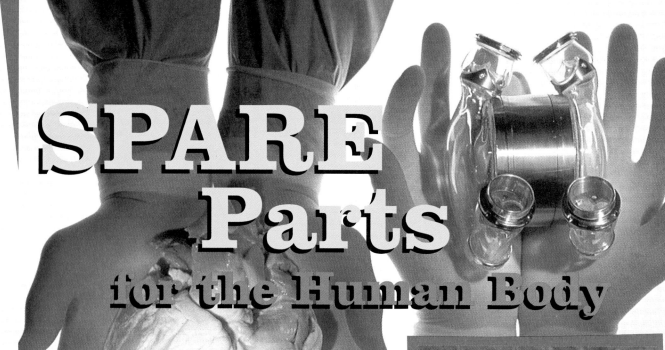

SPARE Parts
for the Human Body

Do you think this artificial heart (above right) looks like a real heart?

This athlete can run, thanks to an artificial leg that bends.

Ever see a peg-legged pirate in a movie? Long ago using wood to replace missing body parts was common. Today we can do better.

Artificial skin can't feel, but it can help the body heal.

People still lose body parts in accidents or because of diseases. These people are given artificial, or manufactured, body parts. Lost teeth can be replaced by implants made with plastic or porcelain. The implants look like real teeth. Arms or legs can be replaced by artificial limbs made of plastic or special metals. These limbs bend and work much like natural ones.

Most organs are harder to replace. Doctors have implanted artificial hearts to replace diseased ones. Since the main function of a heart is to move blood, a small pump was chosen for the job.

However, no pump works as well as a real heart. An artificial heart can't be used for long because it damages cells. After a few days, doctors must transplant a healthy heart into the person's body.

Scientists have also developed artificial skin. It's used mostly for people who've been badly burned. Like an artificial heart, artificial skin isn't meant for permanent use. However, it helps keep germs outside and fluids inside the body while the body heals.

Discussion
Starter

1 Why are bones and teeth easier to replace than organs such as hearts, livers, and lungs?

2 What is the main purpose of using artificial skin?

*inter***NET**
CONNECTION To learn more about artificial body parts, visit www.mhschool.com/science and enter the keyword **SPARE.**

WHY IT MATTERS

Knowing the basic structures of cells helps you tell the difference between plant and animal cells.

SCIENCE WORDS

chloroplast a plant cell's food factory

cell wall a thick, stiff structure that protects and supports a plant cell

vacuole a holding bin for food, water, and wastes

nucleus cell's control center

cell membrane a cell's thin outer covering; found beneath the cell wall in plants

cytoplasm a jellylike substance that fills the cell

chromosome a threadlike structure that controls an organism's traits

Looking at Cells

Have you ever tossed a ball against a wall? It is a fun way to pass the time on a sunny summer afternoon. However, did you ever think about the things around you? What is the wall made of? What are the plants made of? What are YOU made of?

This wall is made up of bricks. The tree and other living things are made up of cells. Compare the person and the tree. How are they alike and different?

EXPLORE

HYPOTHESIZE How could you find out how plant and animal cells are different? Write a hypothesis in your *Science Journal.*

Investigate How Plant and Animal Cells Are Different

Use a microscope to look at plant and animal cells to find out if they are different. The plant cells are from a freshwater plant called *Elodea* (i lō′dē ə). The animal cells are cheek cells that line the inside of a person's mouth.

MATERIALS

- prepared slide of *Elodea* leaf
- prepared slide of human cheek cells
- microscope
- *Science Journal*

PROCEDURES

1. Place the slide of *Elodea* on the microscope stage.

2. **OBSERVE** Focus through the top layers of cells using low power. Focus on one plant cell. Draw it in your *Science Journal*.

3. **OBSERVE** Place the prepared slide of cheek cells on the microscope stage. Focus on one cheek cell using low power. Draw it.

4. **COMMUNICATE** Draw a table like this one. Record your observations.

Characteristics of Plant and Animal Cells

	Shape	Color	Cell Structures Present
Plant cell			
Animal cell			

CONCLUDE AND APPLY

1. **OBSERVE** What did you see when you observed the *Elodea* cells?

2. **OBSERVE** What did you see when you observed the cheek cells?

3. **COMPARE AND CONTRAST** How are the *Elodea* and cheek cells similar and different?

4. **COMPARE AND CONTRAST** How does the *Elodea* cell compare with the onion skin cell you observed in Topic 1?

GOING FURTHER: Apply

5. **INFER** How do you think scientists use cell structure in classifying organisms?

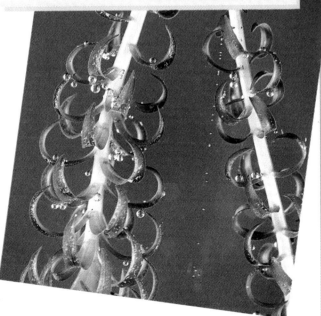

***Elodea* plant**

How Are Plant and Animal Cells Different?

Most cells have everything they need to carry out the five basic life functions. However, as the Explore Activity showed, plant and animal cells are not made up of all the same parts. The diagram on this page shows the major parts of a typical plant cell. The diagram on the next page shows the major parts of a typical animal cell.

Cells also contain some other parts that have specific jobs. One part is like the cell's power plant. Food is burned here to give the cell energy.

Another part of the cell is like a chemical factory. It helps make the cell's building materials.

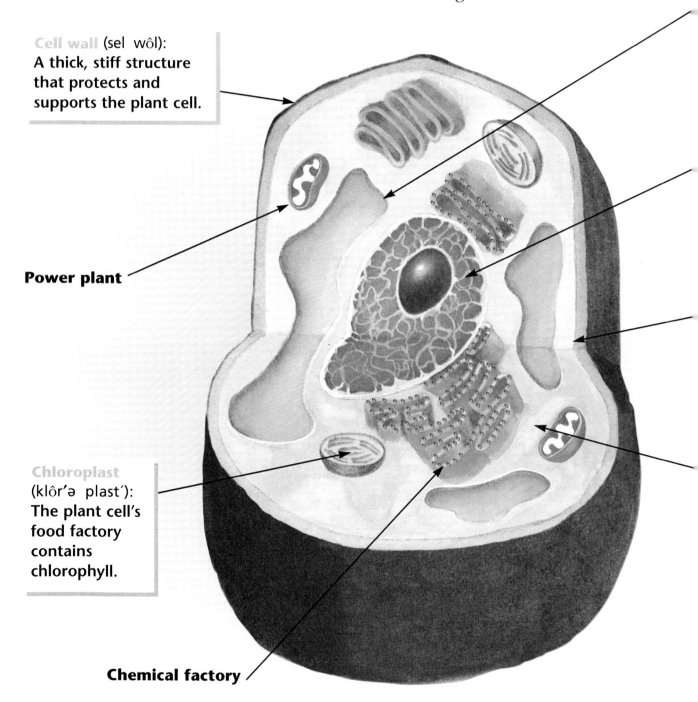

Cell wall (sel wôl):
A thick, stiff structure that protects and supports the plant cell.

Power plant

Chloroplast (klôr′ə plast′):
The plant cell's food factory contains chlorophyll.

Chemical factory

14

Vacuole (vak′ū ōl′):
A holding bin for food, water, and wastes. Plant cells have one or two vacuoles. Vacuoles are small in animal cells. Animal cells have more vacuoles than plant cells.

Power plant

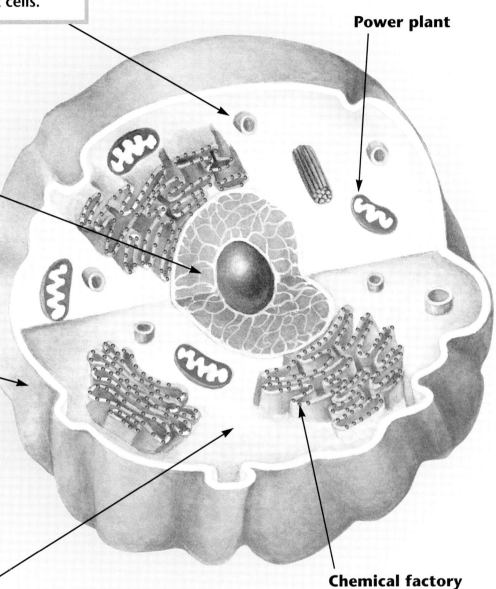

Nucleus
(nü′klē əs):
The nucleus is one of the largest parts of the cell. It controls cell activities.

Cell membrane
(sel mem′brān):
An animal cell's thin outer covering. In plants it is found beneath the cell wall.

Chemical factory

Cytoplasm
(sī′tə plaz′əm):
The jellylike substance that fills the cell. It is mostly water but contains many important chemicals.

READING DIAGRAMS

1. DISCUSS How are the cell wall and cell membrane similar and different?

2. WRITE List the two cell parts that a plant cell has that an animal cell doesn't.

What Do Cell Parts Do?

Different cell parts help carry out the five basic life functions. Each part can be compared with something in the real world.

② The Food Factory: Making Food Chloroplasts are a plant cell's food factories. They contain chlorophyll and use energy from the Sun to make food. Animals get energy from foods they eat.

① The Fences: Protection The cell membrane and cell wall are like fences. Gates, or holes, let in needed materials. Other gates let wastes leave the cell.

③ The Power Plant: Produces Energy Plant and animal cells get energy in the "power plant." It works like an engine to break down fuel, which is food, and releases energy.

⑤ The Copy Shop: Reproduction The nucleus has the master plans for all cell activities. It contains chromosomes (krō′mə sōmz′). Chromosomes are threadlike structures that control an organism's traits. To reproduce, a cell makes a copy of its chromosomes. It splits to form two cells. Each new cell gets a copy of the chromosomes.

④ The Chemical Factory: Growth and Change "Chemical factories" in a cell make building materials. Other parts put the materials together to help the cell grow and change.

⑥ The Holding Bin: Storage A vacuole stores food, water, and wastes.

BREAD BAKING CO.

Brain Power

Is this a model of a plant cell or animal cell? Why do you think so?

Skill: Making a Model

MODELING PLANT AND ANIMAL CELLS

Most cells are too small for you to see without a microscope, but you can build models of cells. Models are three-dimensional copies or drawings of real things. A model can help you see how something looks or behaves.

SAFETY: Do not eat any of the activity materials!

1. **PLAN** In your *Science Journal*, make a list of parts of an animal cell. Name a material to stand for each part.

2. **MAKE A MODEL** Build an animal cell using the materials you named for each part.

3. **REPEAT** Follow the same process for a plant-cell model. How will it be different from your animal-cell model?

4. **COMMUNICATE** Compare your cell models. Record your observations.

CONCLUDE AND APPLY

1. **EXPLAIN** How did building a model help you understand the shape of each type of cell?

2. **OBSERVE** What cell structures do your models have?

3. **COMPARE AND CONTRAST** What structures do both of your models share? What structures don't they share?

4. **INFER** In what ways do you think your cell models are similar to real cells? In what ways are they different?

MATERIALS

- small plastic bags with twist ties
- prepared, light-colored gelatin
- beads or marbles
- green jelly beans or olives
- lima beans
- marshmallows
- clear plastic box
- tape
- scissors
- *Science Journal*

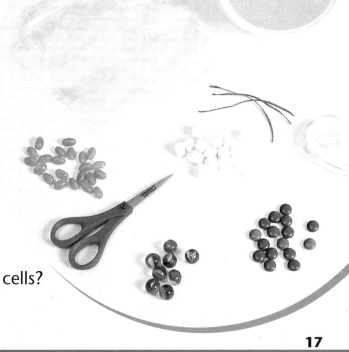

How Can You Compare Plant and Animal Cells?

As the Explore and Skill Builder activities showed, plant and animal cells are different. The basic differences between most plant and animal cells include their covering, color, and shape. Cells also differ depending on the types of jobs they do and the tissues they make up.

What observations did you make of the *Elodea* and human cheek cells? They are alike in some ways. Both are small. Both are filled with a jelly-like substance. Both have outer coverings with small structures inside.

Elodea and human cheek cells are also different in some ways. These are the basic differences between most plant and animal cells:

- **Covering** A plant cell has a thick wall. An animal cell has a thin covering.
- **Color** Most plant cells have green coloring. An animal cell does not.
- **Shape** Most plant cells have a boxy shape. Animal cells have a wide variety of shapes.

As you continue this topic, you will learn more about plant and animal cells. You will also learn about the jobs cell parts have.

THE SHAPE OF A CELL TELLS A LOT ABOUT ITS JOB

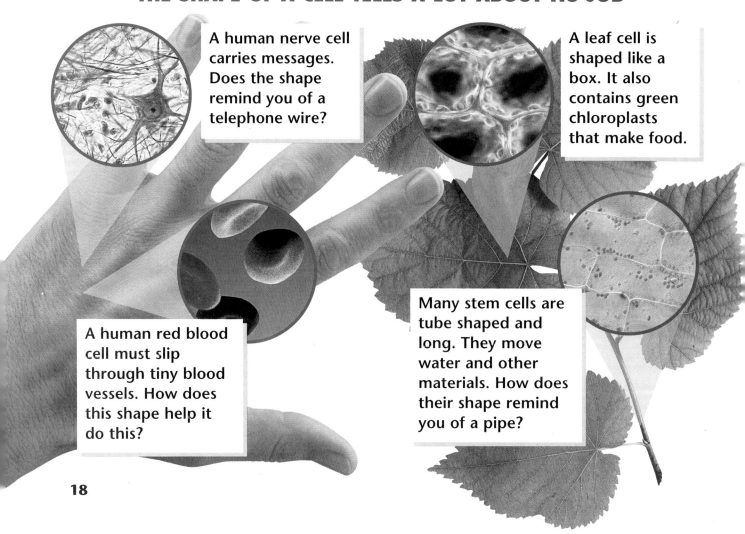

A human nerve cell carries messages. Does the shape remind you of a telephone wire?

A leaf cell is shaped like a box. It also contains green chloroplasts that make food.

A human red blood cell must slip through tiny blood vessels. How does this shape help it do this?

Many stem cells are tube shaped and long. They move water and other materials. How does their shape remind you of a pipe?

Are There Other Types of Cells?

The one-celled microorganisms that live in pond water are called *protists* (prō′tists). Here are some other types of cells and organisms.

Bacteria (bak tîr′ē ə) are one-celled organisms. A bacterium (singular) has a cell wall but no nucleus. The chromosomes are scattered through the cell. Bacteria do not have many cell structures. Bacteria are much smaller than most plant, animal, or protist cells.

A great variety of these microorganisms live on Earth. Some cause illnesses, like strep throat. Many bacteria are helpful. Some are used to make foods like cheese and buttermilk. Some break down waste materials, such as dead plants and animals.

Have you ever eaten a mushroom or used yeast to make bread? These are two examples of *fungi* (fun′jī). Yeast is a one-celled organism. A mushroom is made of many cells. Fungi cells have a cell wall and a nucleus, like plant cells. Some cells even have more than one nucleus.

Fungi do not have green chloroplasts or make food. Some fungi, like mushrooms, absorb nutrients from dead organisms. Have you ever seen a fungus growing on a log in the forest? Along with bacteria, it is breaking down the log and absorbing nutrients from it.

How are fungi cells like animals cells? How are they like plant cells?

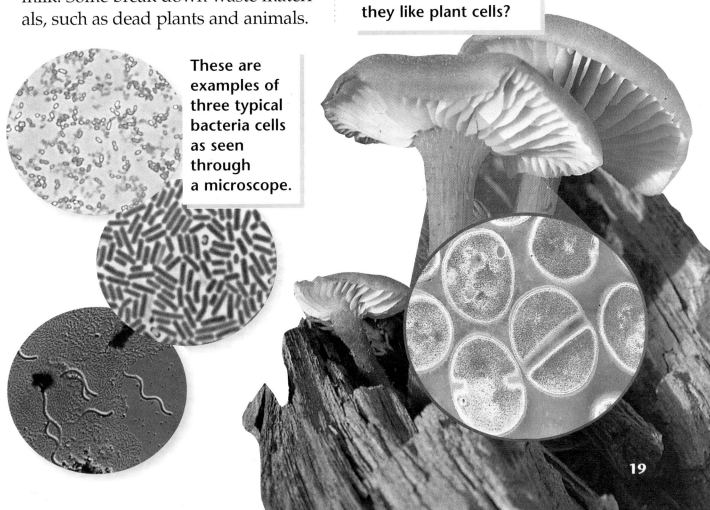

These are examples of three typical bacteria cells as seen through a microscope.

Is It Living?

Viruses (vī'rəs ez) are described as particles. They are much smaller than cells. They can't be seen with a microscope like the one you use. They can be seen only with a very powerful microscope.

A virus is not a cell. A virus is not living. It does not have a nucleus or other cell parts. The only thing a virus contains is a set of plans for invading living cells.

A virus does not make or use food. It does not grow, change, or respond to its environment. The only life function a virus seems to perform is being able to reproduce.

If a virus is not living, how can it reproduce? It cannot reproduce on its own but must use a living cell, as shown here.

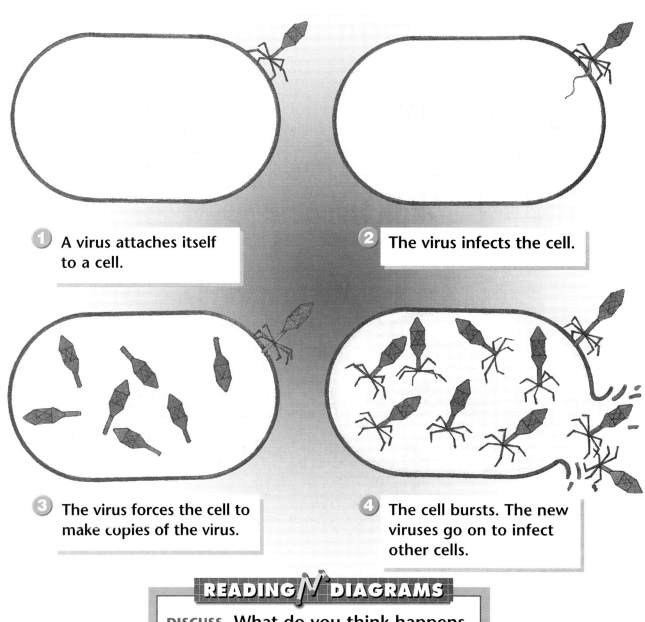

1 A virus attaches itself to a cell.

2 The virus infects the cell.

3 The virus forces the cell to make copies of the virus.

4 The cell bursts. The new viruses go on to infect other cells.

READING ✓ DIAGRAMS

DISCUSS What do you think happens after the cell bursts?

FUNtastic Facts

Nerve cells can be very long. A nerve cell connecting your big toe or your thumb to your spine may be 1 meter long. The longest animal nerve cells are found in a giraffe's leg. They can measure up to 2 meters in length. Why is it important for nerve cells to be so long?

MATH
LINK

WHY IT MATTERS

There are many different types of cells, and there are many types of organisms in the world. Now that you know what a cell looks like and how its parts work, you can identify types of cells. It will also help you understand how organisms are different. For example, plants are different from animals in many ways. That is why plant cells have parts different from animal cells. You will use this knowledge as you learn more about how organisms are classified.

REVIEW

1. How are cells and organisms similar to bricks and buildings?

2. How are plant and animal cells alike and different?

3. Describe the functions of the cell membrane, nucleus, and cytoplasm.

4. MAKE A MODEL What if you made models of bacteria and fungi cells? How would they be different from your model of a plant cell?

5. CRITICAL THINKING *Apply*
A cell has green structures inside. How do you know what kind of cell it is? What kind of outer covering do you think it has?

WHY IT MATTERS THINK ABOUT IT
What if plant cells did not have cell walls? How do you think this would affect a plant?

WHY IT MATTERS WRITE ABOUT IT
What if animal cells had a cell wall? How would this affect them?

LARGER THAN LIFE

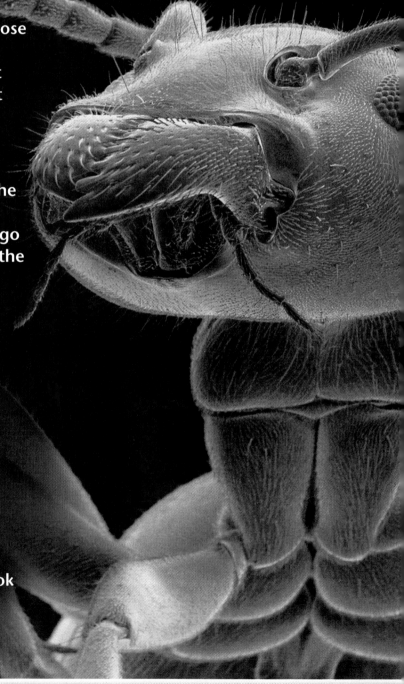

What lets you see things up close and personal? A microscope! It helps you view a tiny world that has a big effect on our lives. If it weren't for the microscope, we wouldn't know about cells, bacteria, or viruses.

A microscope lens is thick in the middle and thin at the edges. When light rays from an object go into the lens, they bend. When the rays reach your eyes, the object looks much larger than it is.

The first microscopes had one lens. They were called simple microscopes. English scientist Robert Hooke looked at cork through a microscope in 1665. What he saw looked like boxes, so he named them cells!

Today we use compound microscopes with two or more lenses. One is near the object. Another is near your eye. The bottom lens makes an object look bigger than it is. The top lens makes it look even bigger!

Physical Science Link

The electron microscope doesn't shine light on an object, and you don't look through lenses to see the object. This microscope hits an object with tiny charged particles. The magnetic lenses pull together a detailed picture of the object!

Scientists use microscopes to search for cures for diseases. They also study plant cells to find out which grow well where it seldom rains—or rains too much!

Microscopes are used for many other tasks. Robert Hooke would be very impressed!

DISCUSSION STARTER

What's the difference between a simple and a compound microscope?

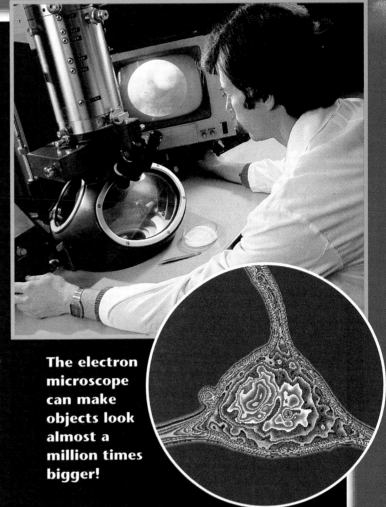

The electron microscope can make objects look almost a million times bigger!

Bent light rays

Lens

Enlarged image

Object

Light rays

Eye

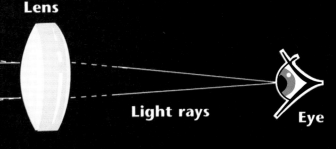

To learn more about microscopes, visit *www.mhschool.com/science* and enter the keyword UPCLOSE.

*inter*NET
CONNECTION

SCIENCE WORDS

cell p. 5
cell
   membrane p. 15
cell wall p. 14
chloroplast p. 14
chromosome p. 16
cytoplasm p. 15

nucleus p. 15
organ p. 6
organism p. 4
organ system p. 6
oxygen p. 4
tissue p. 5
vacuole p. 15

USING SCIENCE WORDS

Number a paper from 1 to 10. Fill in 1 to 5 with words from the list above.

1. The cell structure that holds water, food, and wastes is the ___?___.

2. The thin, outer covering found both in plant and animal cells is the ___?___.

3. A structure in a plant cell that makes food is a(n) ___?___.

4. A group of similar cells that work together to carry out a job form a(n) ___?___.

5. Groups of tissues form a(n) ___?___.

6–10. Pick five words from the list above that were not used in 1 to 5, and use each in a sentence.

UNDERSTANDING SCIENCE IDEAS

11. How is a virus not like an organism that lives in pond water?

12. Why don't animal cells have chloroplasts?

USING IDEAS AND SKILLS

13. **READING SKILL: RECOGNIZE A LIST** Define an organ system and give an example. Make a list of what the organ system would be made of, starting with the cell.

14. **MAKE A MODEL** Draw and label both a plant cell and an animal cell. In your plant cell drawing, circle in red the parts not found in an animal cell.

15. **THINKING LIKE A SCIENTIST** What do you know about how a virus works? How could you use this information to stop a virus that makes people sick?

PROBLEMS and PUZZLES

Living or Nonliving How can you tell if a white spot on a tomato is a living thing? Describe a safe way you could test it to find out.

Are All Plants Alike? Have an adult take you to a nearby park. Use a hand lens to study the plants there. How are the flowers, leaves, and stems alike? Different?

CHAPTER 2
HOW ORGANISMS ARE CLASSIFIED

Can you tell a plant from an animal just by looking? Do you see a plant and an animal here? How can you tell one from the other? Are all living things either an animal or a plant? Is an ant an animal? Is a mushroom a plant? As you read this chapter, you will be able to answer these questions.

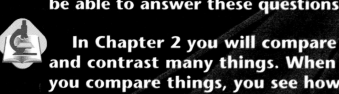 In Chapter 2 you will compare and contrast many things. When you compare things, you see how they are alike. When you contrast things, you see how they are different.

Topic
LIFE SCIENCE
3

WHY IT MATTERS

Classifying organisms helps people to study and learn about living things.

SCIENCE WORDS

kingdom the largest group into which an organism is classified

trait a characteristic of an organism

genus a group made up of two or more very similar species

species the smallest group into which an organism is classified

Classification

Have you ever had to sort, or classify, a group of items? What were they? How did you do it?

Things like toys can be organized into groups. First you have to decide what characteristic to use to define the groups. For example, it could be soft toys or hard toys.

Do you think living things can be organized into groups, too? Why or why not?

EXPLORE

HYPOTHESIZE What characteristics do you think scientists use to classify living things? Write a hypothesis in your *Science Journal.*

Design Your Own Experiment

HOW ARE ORGANISMS CLASSIFIED?

PROCEDURES

MATERIALS

- reference books
- *Science Journal*

1. **OBSERVE** Choose eight very different organisms that you would like to classify and learn more about. You may choose the ones you see here. Record their names in your *Science Journal.*

2. **COLLECT DATA** What would you like to know about your organisms? Where would you look to find the information? Design a table to record the information.

3. **CLASSIFY** Try to place all of the organisms into groups. What characteristics did you use to help you make your choices?

CONCLUDE AND APPLY

1. **IDENTIFY** How many groups were formed? What were the major characteristics of the organisms in each group?

2. **EXPLAIN** What organisms were placed in each group?

3. **COMMUNICATE** Make a list of the characteristics of the organisms in each group.

GOING FURTHER: Apply

4. **REPEAT** Test your classification system by adding a new organism. Does it fit in a group? Why or why not? If not, what changes could you make to your system so that it would fit?

CLASSIFYING ORGANISMS

Kingdom	Number of Cells	Nucleus	Food	Move from Place to Place
Ancient Bacteria Kingdom	one	no	make	some move
True Bacteria Kingdom	one	no	make or obtain	some move
Protist Kingdom	one or many	yes	make or obtain	some move
Fungus Kingdom	one or many	yes	absorb	no
Plant Kingdom	many	yes	make	no
Animal Kingdom	many	yes	eat	yes

READING N CHARTS

1. **WRITE** What organisms can make food? Make a list.
2. **DISCUSS** Why do you think plants and fungi don't need to move?

How Are Organisms Classified?

The Explore Activity shows that one way to classify organisms is by their physical characteristics.

To classify organisms into large groups, scientists also study many other characteristics. They look at body form and how an organism gets food. They observe if it moves from place to place. They also study the number of cells, if the cells have a nucleus, and cell parts. Even an organism's blood and how it grows and develops before it is born are studied.

For many years scientists could not settle on a single classification system. People often used different names to describe the same organism. This often led to confusion. With time a worldwide classification system was developed. It divides organisms into large groups, called **kingdoms** (king'dəmz). Organisms in each kingdom share basic **traits** (trāts). A trait is a characteristic of a living thing. Organisms within a kingdom are similar to one another but are different from organisms in other kingdoms. The chart above shows the basic traits of organisms in each kingdom.

To Which Kingdom Does an Organism Belong?

A chart can help you organize a lot of information. This chart can help you determine what types of organisms belong in each kingdom. Simply ask the following questions.

Brain Power

An organism is made of many cells, and each cell has a nucleus. It eats food and moves. To which kingdom does it belong?

DOES THE ORGANISM . . .	IF YES, . . .	IF NO, . . .
. . . have a nucleus?	. . . it can be an animal, plant, fungus, or protist.	. . . it can be a true bacterium or ancient bacterium.
. . . have many cells?	. . . it can be an animal, plant, protist, or fungus.	. . . it can be a true bacterium, ancient bacterium, fungus, or protist.
. . . eat or obtain food?	. . . it can be an animal, fungus, or true bacterium.	. . . it can be a true bacterium, ancient bacterium, plant, or protist.
. . . move?	. . . it can be an animal, protist, true bacterium, or ancient bacterium.	. . . it can be a true bacterium, ancient bacterium, protist, plant, or fungus.

How Can Organisms Be Classified Further?

Mountain lions and houseflies belong to the animal kingdom even though they are very different. That is why scientists use smaller and smaller groups to further classify organisms. The smaller the group, the more similar the organisms in it are to each other.

There are seven groups into which an organism can be classified. This chart shows the groups from largest to smallest. There are fewer different kinds of organisms in each group as you move down from the kingdom level.

Kingdom
Members of the animal kingdom move in some way, eat food, and reproduce.

Phylum
A *phylum* is a large group within a kingdom. Members share at least one major characteristic, like having a backbone.

Class
A phylum is broken down into smaller groups, called *classes*. Members of this class all produce milk for their young.

Order
A class is made up of smaller groups, called *orders*. Members of this order are meat eaters.

Family
An order is made up of still smaller groups of similar organisms. These groups are called *families*. Dogs, wolves, and coyotes belong to the same family.

Genus
A family is made up of organisms belonging to similar, even smaller groups. Each group is called a genus. Dogs and wolves belong to the same genus.

Species
The smallest classification group is a species. A species is made up of only one type of organism that can reproduce only with another organism of the same species. All dogs belong to the same species.

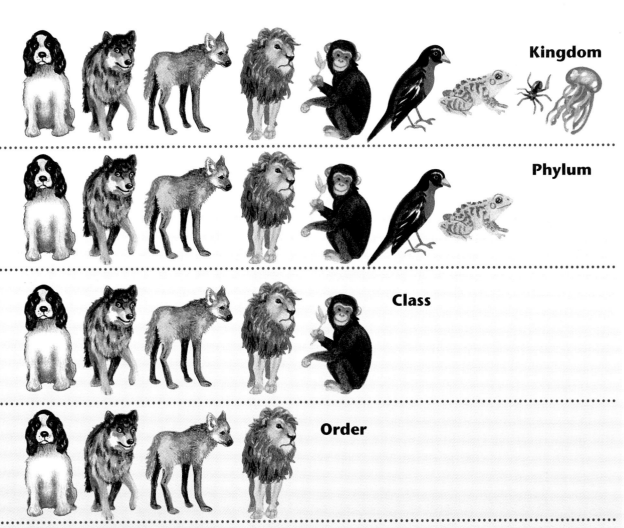

Kingdom

Phylum

Class

Order

Family

Genus

Species

READING /\/ CHARTS

1. **DISCUSS** Are there more organisms in a class or a family? How can you tell?
2. **REPRESENT** Design another chart that shows how the groups are organized. How is it different?

Skill: Classifying

CLASSIFYING LEAVES

When you organize toys or living things into groups, you are classifying. When you classify, you organize things into smaller groups based on their traits. This skill is important not only in science. People classify things every day. Classifying helps make things easier to study and understand. To practice this skill, you will classify leaves according to different traits.

MATERIALS

- 10 leaves or leaf pictures
- ruler
- reference books
- *Science Journal*

PROCEDURES

1. OBSERVE Spread out the leaves (or leaf pictures). Observe the traits they share, such as size, color, shape, and so on. Record the traits in your *Science Journal*.

2. CLASSIFY Choose one trait, such as color, that you recorded in your *Science Journal*. Organize all ten leaves based on that trait. Draw the way your leaves are organized. You may use a table.

3. REPEAT Follow the same procedure for two other traits you recorded.

CONCLUDE AND APPLY

1. IDENTIFY In how many different ways were you able to classify the leaves?

2. COMPARE AND CONTRAST How did your classification system differ from other students' systems? In what ways were they similar?

3. CLASSIFY Give some examples of how other things are classified. Use a kitchen, bedroom, closet, or supermarket.

4. DRAW CONCLUSIONS How do you think using a worldwide classification system might help scientists identify and understand organisms?

How Are Organisms Named?

The classification system helps classify organisms into smaller and smaller groups. It also plays a part in how each organism is named. The naming system that we use today was developed in the 1700s by a Swedish scientist, Carolus Linnaeus.

The first part of an organism's name uses that organism's genus (jē'nəs) name. Remember, a genus is a group made up of two or more very similar species. The second part of its name uses its species (spē'shēz) name. Remember, a species is the smallest classification group. It is made up of only one type of organism that can reproduce only with another organism of the same species.

For example, the genus name for a lion is *Panthera*. A number of large cats share this genus name. However, only the lion has the full name *Panthera leo*.

Yipes!

Using both the genus and species names lets scientists identify specific organisms. For example, the table shows two members of the small cat genus, *Felis*. Which would you rather have curl up in your lap?

Common Name	Genus Name	Species Name
Jaguar	*Panthera*	*onca*
Tiger	*Panthera*	*tigris*
Lion	*Panthera*	*leo*
Mountain lion	*Felis*	*concolor*
House cat	*Felis*	*catus*

33

Are There Organisms That Have Never Been Classified?

Scientists have named and described about 1.75 million species on Earth so far. However, scientists are always looking for organisms that have never been described or classified. Some scientists estimate that we may be sharing the world with 5 million to 15 million species. Many of these species live in tropical rain forests.

Rain Forest Organisms

Scientists are working to find and classify rain forest organisms never seen before. Who knows what interesting and helpful organisms are just waiting to be discovered!

There are many reasons to study rain forest organisms, such as finding new types of medicines. Unfortunately more than 50 acres of rain forest are being cleared every minute for farming and timber.

Red-Eyed Green Tree Frog

Emerald Tree Boa

Red-Breasted Toucan

These are just a few of the thousands of different organisms that live in the rain forest.

These changes affect organisms. If plants that an animal depends on for food or shelter are destroyed, the animal may die. If this continues for a long time, a species may die. That is why scientists are trying to gather information about rain forest organisms as quickly as they can.

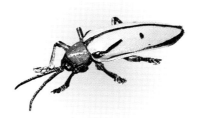

There are more than 300,000 different beetles on Earth. Imagine trying to tell one beetle from another without a classification system!

Classifying organisms helps people in three ways. First, it allows them to keep track of organisms. Second, classification helps people communicate by using one naming system. Finally, classification helps to organize information about organisms for further studies. Studying groups helps people see the "big picture" of how life is organized.

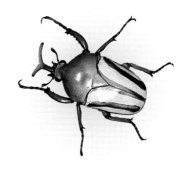

REVIEW

1. Name the different kingdoms. What are the key traits of organisms in each kingdom?

2. Describe how a kingdom is divided into smaller groups.

3. What do scientific names provide that common names do not provide?

4. **CLASSIFY** List and classify ten organisms. What traits did you use? How many groups did you create? Did any organisms not fit into one of the groups? Explain.

5. **CRITICAL THINKING** *Evaluate* How might the extinction of one organism affect others?

WHY IT MATTERS THINK ABOUT IT Prairie dogs are not dogs. Jellyfish are not fish. How do you think using scientific names instead of common names helps prevent misconceptions?

WHY IT MATTERS WRITE ABOUT IT List at least three things that have different names in different parts of the country, for example, soda and pop.

HELPING ONE ANOTHER

Could there be life on Earth without plants? Without animals? Even if there could, how would one survive without the other?

Plants provide most of the food animals eat. Animals also use plants and trees for shelter. Humans also make medicines from plant parts.

The colorings of some animals blend in with the plants around them. Some animals use plants to hide and store food. Plants even produce oxygen for animals to breathe!

Plants do a lot for animals, but some plants need animals, too. When bees eat nectar from flowers, they pollinate flowers. Pollen is a dustlike material needed to grow new plants. As a bee feeds, pollen grains stick to its body. Then when the bee flies to another flower, it deposits some pollen there.

The pollen helps form new seeds so new flowers can grow!

Some animals eat fruits of plants but can't digest the seeds. These are later passed through the body and deposited somewhere else. Other seeds cling to an animal's fur and fall off later in some other area. If plant seeds just fall, a garden becomes too crowded for every plant to grow. Animals help put seeds where they'll have a chance to grow.

Some plants need animals as food! The leaves of a Venus's-flytrap snap shut to catch insects that land. The bladderwort traps insects in pouches on its underground roots!

DISCUSSION STARTER

1. Why do you think some plants need insects for food?

2. How do humans help plants spread their seeds around?

To learn more about the relationships of plants and animals, visit *www.mhschool.com/science* and enter the keyword HELP.

inter**NET**
CONNECTION

WHY IT MATTERS

Learning about the past helps us learn about the present.

SCIENCE WORDS

fossil any evidence of an organism that lived in the past

embryo an undeveloped animal or plant

extinct describes an organism that is no longer alive on Earth

Classifying Organisms of the Past

How much do we know about the great meat-eating dinosaur *Tyrannosaurus rex?* It was 14 meters (46 feet) long and 6 meters (20 feet) tall, and it weighed 8 tons (17,600 pounds). It walked upright on two powerful legs. Its tiny arms were really too short even to reach its mouth. How do we know so much about *T. rex?* The evidence it left behind tells us.

EXPLORE

HYPOTHESIZE Does this dinosaur skeleton remind you of any animals alive today? What might be learned from comparing the bones of past and present-day animals? Write a hypothesis in your *Science Journal.*

Investigate Using Skeletons to Compare Organisms

Carefully observe and compare the three skeletons.

MATERIALS

- ruler, pencil, and paper, or computer with charting program
- *Science Journal*

PROCEDURES

1. **COMPARE AND CONTRAST** Compare the picture of the dinosaur skeleton on page 38 with the skeletons on this page.

2. **COMMUNICATE** Make a chart in your *Science Journal* that lists the similarities and differences. Use the computer if you like.

CONCLUDE AND APPLY

1. **IDENTIFY** Write a paragraph about the similarities and differences you noticed among the skeletons.

GOING FURTHER: Apply

2. **DRAW CONCLUSIONS** What types of things can be learned by comparing the skeletons of present-day animals with the skeletons of animals of the past?

This is a skeleton of a bird.

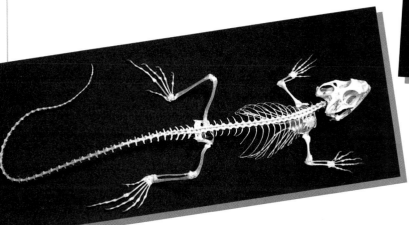

This is a skeleton of a reptile.

39

How Are Skeletons Used to Compare Organisms?

A **fossil** (fos′əl) is any evidence of an organism that lived in the past. Fossils are often skeletons preserved in rock. When someone discovers a new fossil, he or she might wonder, "How would the organism that made this fit into today's classification system?" As in the Explore Activity, he or she might compare the fossil with bones of similar animals living today.

Many people are interested in the history of organisms that lived in the past. They might also study an organism of today and wonder what its ancestors were like. Finding this type of information is something like filling in a family tree.

As scientists try to learn more about an organism's past, they must consider that organisms change over time. Change in living things over time is called *evolution* (ev′ə lü′shən).

For example, using fossils of skulls, teeth, and leg bones, scientists have traced the ancestors of the modern horse back about 60 million years. The diagram on the right shows only some of the ancestors of the horse. The first ancestor was about the size of a small dog. How do the leg bones of today's horse compare with its ancestor's bones?

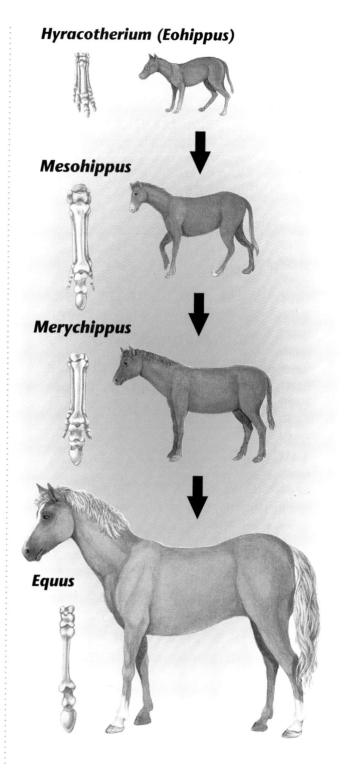

Hyracotherium (Eohippus)

Mesohippus

Merychippus

Equus

Based on fossil evidence, scientists think *Hyracotherium (Eohippus)* is the ancestor of all horses. What similarities and differences do you see? How did the animals' appearance and leg structure change?

What Does Other Fossil Evidence Tell You?

Another thing that we can learn is the age of a fossil compared with other fossils. This can be done by studying the rock layer in which a fossil is found.

How do you think studying rock layers tells you about a fossil's age? Looking at other fossils found in the same rock layer tells that the organisms lived at about the same time. The oldest fossils are in the oldest rock layers, which are at the bottom. Younger fossils are found in later, upper rock layers. These fossils are younger than fossils in lower layers.

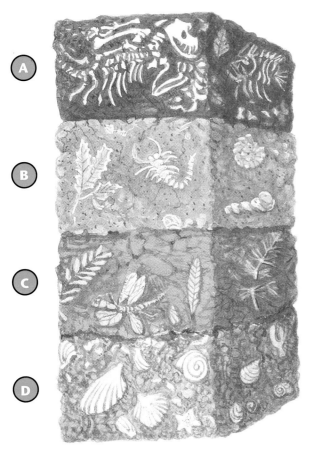

Fossils found in layer A are younger than fossils found in layer B. Which rock layer contains fossils older than layer C?

QUICK LAB

Older and Younger

MATERIALS
- 4 books
- 2 pieces of paper
- scissors
- pen or pencil
- *Science Journal*

HYPOTHESIZE **Relative dating is placing things in order from oldest to youngest. What do you look for to help you decide which is older and younger? Write a hypothesis in your** *Science Journal.*

PROCEDURES

1. **OBSERVE** Cut a piece of paper into four pieces. Draw a "fossil" on each piece. Place one fossil inside the front cover of each book. Stack the books.

2. **INTERPRET DATA** Challenge your partner to find the fossils and arrange them in order of which is "oldest" and "youngest." Record any observations you make in your *Science Journal.*

3. **REPEAT** Switch roles and repeat the activity.

CONCLUDE AND APPLY

1. **EXPLAIN** What did the books represent?

2. **IDENTIFY** Which fossil was oldest? Youngest? What evidence helped you decide?

41

Can Organisms That Seem Different Be Related?

What do you think the organisms on this page have in common? Do their limb bones seem similar to you in any ways?

Even though each animal uses these bones differently, the bones are arranged in similar ways. Scientists compare limbs to understand what is similar and different about organisms. They can see which have similar features and might be related.

Scientists use the evidence shown by limb bones when they classify organisms. Some of their findings are surprising. For example, whales are more closely related to humans than to sharks! You can see this by looking at whale flipper bones. They are much more like human arm bones than shark fins. Whales and humans are both mammals.

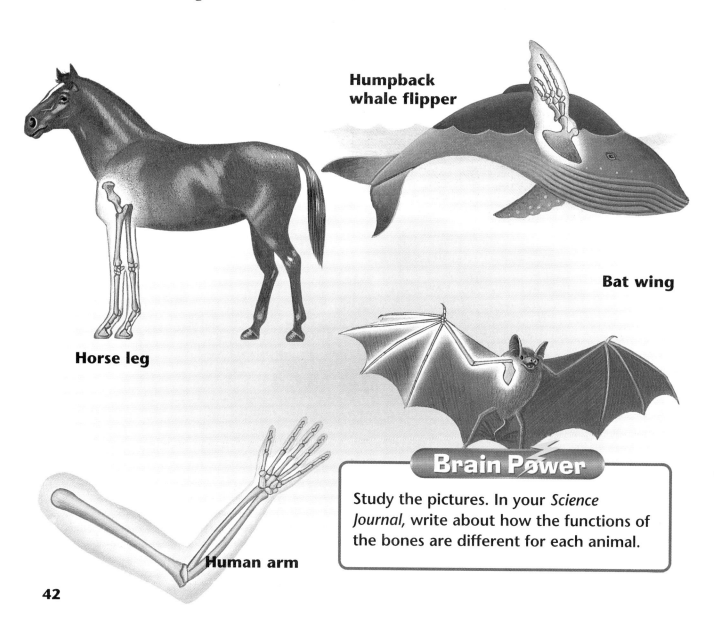

Humpback whale flipper

Bat wing

Horse leg

Human arm

Brain Power

Study the pictures. In your *Science Journal*, write about how the functions of the bones are different for each animal.

What Are Some Other Clues?

Another clue to finding similarities among organisms comes from before they were even born. An undeveloped animal or plant is called an embryo (em'brē ō').

EMBRYOS

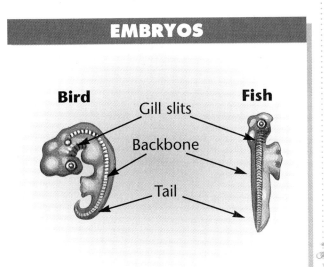

Bird   **Fish**
Gill slits
Backbone
Tail

What do you notice as you compare these two embryos? Each has a backbone, or a spine. They all have gill slits and a tail. These features suggest that the organisms are related. They are all vertebrates.

An embryo changes before it is ready for the world. Some features are lost in certain animals as the embryo grows. Birds do not have gill slits when they are born.

Many organisms are extinct (ek stingkt'), or no longer alive on Earth. To help classify them, scientists can compare fossil embryos with each other and with modern embryos.

Still another clue that organisms might be related can be found in "leftover" structures. Humans don't need a tail, but a human adult has a tailbone at the end of the spine. Some snakes have tiny hip and limb bones. A baleen whale has small, useless hip bones. These useless bones are clues that help classify organisms into groups. That means they are probably related to organisms that have and use those bones.

This blind salamander lives in deep, dark caves. Yet it has useless eyes that don't see. What conclusions can you draw about this salamander's ancestors?

These animals are extinct.

Woolly mammoth

Dusty seaside sparrow

Dodo bird

Why Do Organisms Become Extinct?

Many organisms are extinct. Some scientists believe that 99 out of every 100 species that have ever lived on Earth are extinct.

Judging from fossils, there have been many *mass extinctions*. A mass extinction is when many different species die out at about the same time. The best-known mass extinction is that of the dinosaurs. They died out 65 million years ago, along with more than half of all other animal and plant species.

Some scientists believe that a giant comet hit Earth and caused the extinction of the dinosaurs. Walter Alvarez, along with his father, Dr. Luis Alvarez, found evidence to support the comet theory. The comet would have created great clouds of dust that blocked sunlight. This would have caused dark and cold periods.

Without sunlight, plants could not have made the food they needed to survive. Without plants, plant-eating dinosaurs would have died. Without them, meat-eating dinosaurs would have died.

Other scientists believe that many huge volcanoes erupted, creating great clouds of dust. Still others think that dinosaurs spread deadly diseases as they moved about Earth. Dinosaurs may also have eaten plants that other species depended on, causing them to starve and die. Maybe many events together caused the dinosaur's extinction.

Can People Cause Extinction?

Do you think people can cause extinction? As a matter of fact, people play a big role in extinction. People use pesticides and chemicals, destroy places where animals live, and use up resources. They also hunt and fish. This causes many species to become endangered, or in danger of becoming extinct.

Condors are an endangered species.

WHY IT MATTERS

In a way, learning about the past helps us learn about the present. Knowing how organisms have changed over time and who their ancestors were helps us to better understand the history of life on Earth. It also helps us classify living and extinct organisms.

People today are often interested in their past. They research family history and learn about ancestors. This helps them learn about where their families came from and how they changed over time.

REVIEW

1. What kinds of clues do fossils give about organisms of the past?

2. Is a fossil older or younger than another fossil in a lower rock layer? Explain.

3. How do embryos help identify a common ancestor of different organisms?

4. **COMMUNICATE** Explain some possible causes of dinosaur extinction. What are some causes of extinction today?

5. **CRITICAL THINKING** *Analyze* Some snakes have tiny hip and limb bones. What does this tell you about their ancestors? What traits might you find in the group they once belonged to?

WHY IT MATTERS THINK ABOUT IT Why do you think it is interesting for people to learn about their ancestors?

WHY IT MATTERS WRITE ABOUT IT What types of questions would you ask if you could talk to one of your ancestors? Why?

READING SKILL Write about how you can compare and contrast organisms of today with organisms of the past.

SCIENCE MAGAZINE

Helping Endangered Species

Ever wish that you could help endangered animals and plants? Some kids in Hawaii did, so they found a way to help! Students at the Enchanted Lake Elementary School wanted to help as many endangered species as they could—in Hawaii and elsewhere around the world. The kids started Project Lokahi. *Lokahi* is Hawaiian for "harmony."

With help from the students of Enchanted Lake, some organisms might not end up as "things of the past!"

Kids Did It!

Many species in Hawaii had no natural enemies. Without enemies they lost their defenses over time. For example, the Hawaiian raspberry lost its thorns, and some birds lost the ability to fly.

People brought predators to Hawaii from other parts of the world, such as mongooses, rats, Argentine ants, and wild pigs. These predators greatly harmed the bird and plant populations of the islands. Foreign plants were also harmful. The South American banana poka (pō′kə) and the miconia (mī cō′nē ə) are two vines that suffocated native plants.

To help endangered species, the kids set up a Web page on the Internet. There they explain which animals are in trouble and where the animals live. For example, the Web page lists the green sea turtle. At one time people hunted these turtles for their eggs,

Kauai
Niihau
Oahu
Molokai
Maui
Lani
Kahoolawe
PACIFIC OCEAN
Hawaiian Islands
Hawaii

meat, and shells. Green sea turtles lay their eggs on beaches in North Carolina and other warm places.

After learning about the turtles, people might help to protect them. People might put signs on the beaches or post fliers to warn people when the turtles are laying their eggs.

DISCUSSION STARTER

1. What kinds of information would convince people to protect endangered species?

2. Why do you think the kids chose the name Lokahi for the project?

Sea turtles need a safe place to lay their eggs.

To learn more about endangered species, visit *www.mhschool.com/science* and enter the keyword ATRISK.

*inter*NET
CONNECTION

WHY IT MATTERS

Living and nonliving things depend on one another.

SCIENCE WORDS

ecosystem living and non-living things in an environment and how they interact

community the living part of an ecosystem

population one type of organism living in an area

habitat an organism's home

producer an organism that makes food

consumer an organism that eats food

decomposer an organism that breaks down wastes and the remains of other organisms

food chain shows the set of steps in which organisms get the food they need to survive

food web shows the pattern of how food chains in an ecosystem are related

Organisms and Where They Live

What types of organisms live in deserts? Deserts are the driest places on Earth. In some deserts the amount of rain in a year would make a puddle only the thickness of a few pages in this book. During the day some deserts sizzle at temperatures above 45°C (113°F). Surprisingly some animals and plants make their homes in deserts. How do they survive? In fact how do living things in any environment survive?

EXPLORE

HYPOTHESIZE The key to an organism's survival is how it interacts with other living and nonliving things. What might these interactions be? Write a hypothesis in your *Science Journal.* Test it.

This is a kit fox.

EXPLORE ACTIVITY

Investigate How Living and Nonliving Things Interact

MATH LINK

Build a terrarium as a model of an environment. Observe it to see how living things interact with each other and their surroundings.

PROCEDURES

Safety Be careful with live animals.

1. **MAKE A MODEL** Landscape your terrarium. Put taller plants in the back. Spread grass seed and any rocks, twigs, or other things you like.

2. If you add small animals, such as earthworms, sow bugs, and snails, add a water dish.

3. **MEASURE** In your *Science Journal*, make a data table. Record the height of each plant. Measure the plants in two weeks, and record the data. Make a bar graph.

4. Place the terrarium in a lighted area. Avoid direct sunlight.

5. **COMMUNICATE** Draw a diagram of your terrarium. Draw arrows to show how the organisms depend on each other.

CONCLUDE AND APPLY

1. **CLASSIFY** What are the living and nonliving things in the terrarium?

2. **INFER** Why should the terrarium not be placed in direct sunlight?

GOING FURTHER: Apply

3. **OBSERVE** Continue to maintain and observe your terrarium. Did anything unusual happen? Why do you think this happened?

MATERIALS

- prepared terrarium container
- small plants and animals
- plastic spoon
- ruler
- water mister
- grass seeds, rocks, twigs, sticks, bark, dried grass
- *Science Journal*

49

How Do Living and Nonliving Things Interact?

The terrarium in the Explore Activity is a model of an ecosystem (ek′ō sis′təm). Ecosystems include both living and nonliving things. The nonliving part of your ecosystem included water, pebbles, air, light, and soil. The living part of the ecosystem included the plants and animals. The study of how living and nonliving things interact is called *ecology* (ē kol′ə jē).

The living part of an ecosystem forms a community (kə mū′ni tē). Each ecosystem has its own community. The terrarium community had small plants and animals. A desert community includes beautiful cacti and deadly scorpions.

Do you think the members of a community can be grouped further? Communities can be divided into different populations (pop′yə lā′shənz). A population is made of only one type of organism. Your terrarium ecosystem had populations of organisms such as snails and earthworms.

Each organism's home is called its habitat (hab′i tat′). An earthworm lives in a soil habitat. A whale's habitat is the ocean. A termite's habitat is a termite nest.

What makes up the community in this ecosystem?

This diagram will help you understand the different parts of an ecosystem.

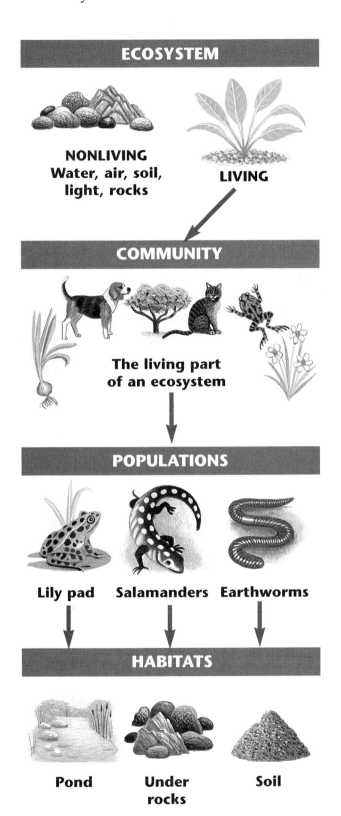

ECOSYSTEM

NONLIVING
Water, air, soil, light, rocks

LIVING

COMMUNITY

The living part of an ecosystem

POPULATIONS

Lily pad   Salamanders   Earthworms

HABITATS

Pond   Under rocks   Soil

QUICK LAB

A Misty Experiment

HYPOTHESIZE What kinds of habitats do different organisms prefer? Form a hypothesis. Use your terrarium to find out.

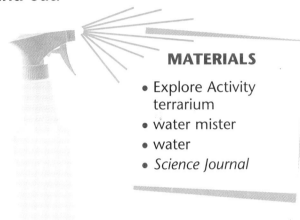

MATERIALS

- Explore Activity terrarium
- water mister
- water
- *Science Journal*

PROCEDURES

1. Lightly spray one side of your terrarium each day for one week. Leave the other side dry.

2. OBSERVE In your *Science Journal*, record your observations of how the organisms react each day.

CONCLUDE AND APPLY

1. PREDICT Which organisms preferred the wet side of the terrarium? Where would you expect these organisms to live in the wild? Explain.

2. PREDICT Which organisms preferred the dry side of the terrarium? Where would you expect these organisms to live in the wild? Explain.

How Are Ecosystems Different?

What makes one ecosystem different from another? In many cases water is the key. A desert is very dry. Only a small number of species of plants and animals can survive with little water. A rain forest has plenty of water. That is why it can support a great variety of plants and animals.

Another resource that can affect ecosystems is sunlight. Some plants, like cacti, grow where there is little water but plenty of sunlight. These types of plants could not grow in an area where there is little sunlight, even if there is plenty of water.

Still another resource is soil. Areas with soil that has many nutrients can support many plants. Few plants grow in areas with soil that does not have many nutrients.

How are all these plants similar and different? What factors affect the types of plants that grow in these ecosystems?

These plants grow in a desert.

52

The types of plants and animals that live in a particular ecosystem depend on a combination of these things. For example, a woodland forest has enough water and rich enough soil for grasses to grow. However, it does not have enough sunshine for most types of grasses. Too much of the Sun's light is blocked by the trees. The forest floor is so dark that most kinds of grasses can't grow there.

Organisms Change the Environment

In all types of ecosystems organisms cause changes. Most changes do not affect the ecosystem very much. When plants and animals move, eat, and grow, they are usually just doing their part to keep the system in balance.

Some changes can harm the environment. Too many animals in one area may use up all the food or water. Humans may harm the environment by building houses on forest or desert land.

Other changes improve and protect the ecosystem. Plants keep the soil in an ecosystem from eroding. Birds may eat insects that would harm plants in the environment. Humans protect animals by setting up wildlife preserves.

These plants grow in a rain forest.

What Types of Roles Do Organisms Play?

A community works like a team. Each member of the team has its own job to do. There are three different types of team members.

Producers (prə dü′sərz) make food. Consumers (kən sü′mərz) use the food that producers make or eat other organisms. Decomposers (dē′kəm pō′zərz) break down wastes and the remains of other organisms.

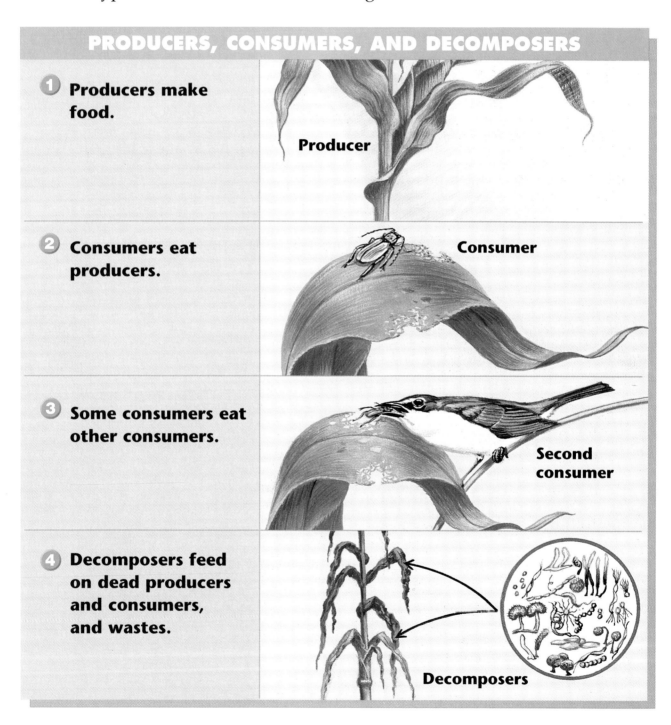

PRODUCERS, CONSUMERS, AND DECOMPOSERS

1. Producers make food.

    Producer

2. Consumers eat producers.

    Consumer

3. Some consumers eat other consumers.

    Second consumer

4. Decomposers feed on dead producers and consumers, and wastes.

    Decomposers

54

What Are Producers?

How do you think you can identify a producer? You can tell most producers by their green color. The color shows that their cells have chloroplasts. Chloroplasts are the cell's "food factories" you learned about in Topic 2. To make food, producers use water, air, simple chemicals, and the Sun's energy.

Producers are the "energy capturers" of the world. They capture light energy from the Sun and transform it into food. Producers use only some of the food they make for themselves. Most of the food goes to other members of the community that eat producers, and organisms that eat them.

Producers Affect Their Environment

Producers are important to many parts of the ecosystem. Without producers there would be no way for other organisms to survive. Consumers and decomposers would not have a valuable source of energy.

Producers also affect nonliving parts of the ecosystem. Plant roots hold the soil in place. Other producers provide shelter for consumers and decomposers. Most producers contribute to the air that we breathe.

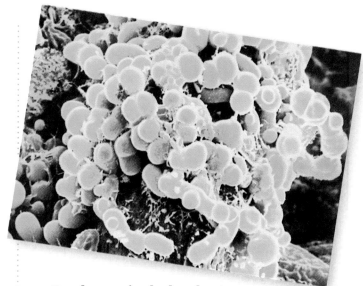

Producers include plants and some kinds of one-celled organisms, like these algae.

Brain Power

What do you think would happen if many producers in a community suddenly died?

What Are Consumers and Decomposers?

Producers are only the beginning of the food chain (füd chān). A food chain is the steps in which organisms get the food they need to survive. Producers make their own food. Consumers and decomposers must get food from producers or other consumers.

Consumers

Which organisms do you think were consumers in the terrarium? Organisms that eat food are consumers. Consumers include animals and some kinds of one-celled organisms. Consumers in the terrarium may have included insects and frogs.

To stay alive, consumers must get food from other organisms. There are three types of consumers. Consumers that eat only plants are called *herbivores*. Other consumers eat only animals. They are called *carnivores*. Consumers that eat plants and animals are called *ominvores*. Which type of consumer are you?

Decomposers

Decomposers in the terrarium may have included microorganisms such as bacteria and some kinds of fungi. They may also have included

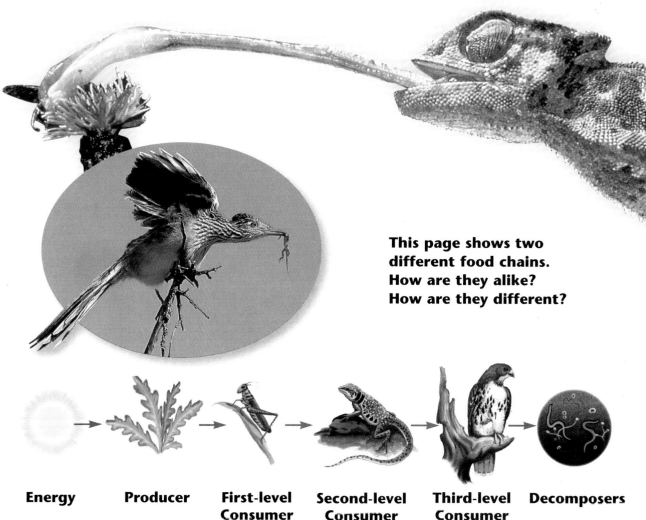

This page shows two different food chains. How are they alike? How are they different?

| Energy | Producer | First-level Consumer | Second-level Consumer | Third-level Consumer | Decomposers |

larger organisms such as worms and snails. Decomposers break down living and dead matter into simple chemicals that they use for food. The chemicals left behind by decomposers are recycled, or used over and over again. Producers use these chemicals for making food.

Have you ever seen mold? Molds are a type of decomposer that often spoils food. Where do molds grow?

The largest animals on Earth, blue whales, are toothless consumers. Their jaws are lined with hundreds of thin plates that strain out from ocean water tiny living things such as algae and tiny sea animals. If there were no algae, could the whales survive? Why or why not?

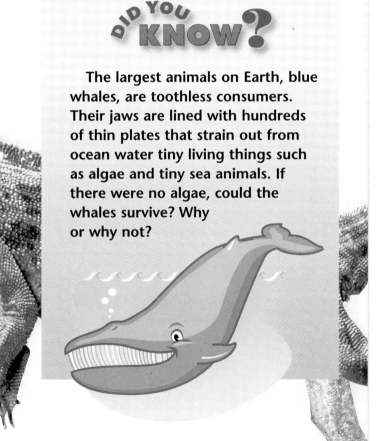

Observe a Decomposer

HYPOTHESIZE What do you think molds need to grow? Write a hypothesis.

MATERIALS

- 5 sealable plastic bags
- 4 food samples
- piece of cardboard
- warm water
- hand lens
- marking pen
- *Science Journal*

PROCEDURES

SAFETY: Do not open the bags after you seal them.

1. Moisten the food samples. Place each in a labeled plastic bag. Put a piece of cardboard in a bag.

2. Seal the bags, and place them in a warm, dark place.

3. **OBSERVE** In your *Science Journal*, record your daily observations.

CONCLUDE AND APPLY

1. **OBSERVE** On which samples did mold grow?

2. **INFER** Will molds grow on any type of material? Explain how the cardboard helped you answer this question.

3. **OBSERVE** How did the molds change the foods?

What is a food web?

Food chains show how energy is passed from the Sun to producers, consumers, and decomposers. In any ecosystem many food chains overlap. Different food chains may include some of the same organisms. Several consumers may all eat the same kind of plant or animal for food. When this happens the food chains form a food web (füd web). A food web shows how food chains are related within an ecosystem.

FOOD WEB

READING /\/ DIAGRAMS

1. **WRITE** Look for a consumer that is in several food chains. Describe the food chains that consumer is part of.
2. **DISCUSS** What might happen to this food web if the hawk begins to die out from a disease?

An ecosystem is made of many parts, including you! Each part depends on the other. Producers, consumers, and decomposers all change the environment around them. Most changes do not seriously affect the ecosystem. Sometimes organisms harm the environment by destroying or using too much of a resource. Organisms can help their ecosystem by doing their jobs and using resources carefully.

How are these people helping to preserve an ecosystem?

REVIEW

1. Describe how the living organisms in the terrarium interacted with the nonliving things and each other.

2. Explain the relationships among an ecosystem, community, population, and habitat.

3. Draw a diagram of an ecosystem. Include the terms *community, population, habitat, producers, consumers,* and *decomposers.*

4. **INFER** What are the advantages and disadvantages of organisms being part of a food web?

5. **CRITICAL THINKING** *Evaluate* Could an ecosystem exist without (a) producers, (b) consumers, (c) decomposers? Explain.

WHY IT MATTERS THINK ABOUT IT
Ecosystems can be found almost anywhere you look—even in your schoolyard! What are some things you can do to preserve an ecosystem?

WHY IT MATTERS WRITE ABOUT IT
Describe one ecosystem that you observed. What living and nonliving things did it include? How did they interact?

SAVED BY THE SUN

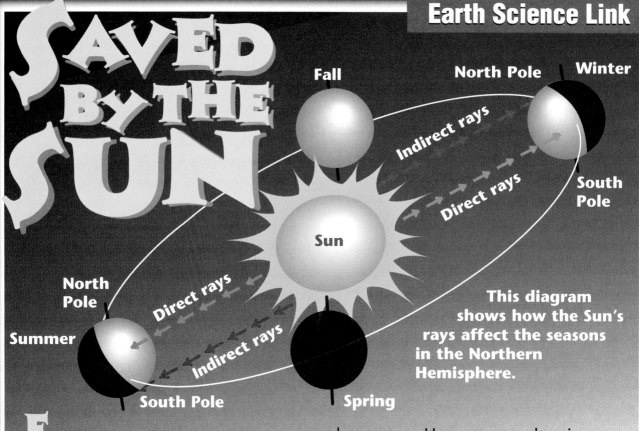

Fall

North Pole

Winter

Indirect rays

Direct rays

South Pole

Sun

North Pole

Direct rays

Summer

Indirect rays

South Pole

Spring

This diagram shows how the Sun's rays affect the seasons in the Northern Hemisphere.

Everything on Earth depends on the Sun. Without it producers couldn't grow. Consumers would starve. Without producers and consumers, decomposers would starve, too.

Earth is saved by the Sun's energy. At any one time, different parts of Earth receive different amounts of solar energy. Places facing the Sun receive its direct rays. Other places get indirect rays that provide less energy. How warm a place is depends on how much solar energy reaches it.

People can collect solar energy and use it to heat their homes. Using solar energy helps save natural resources such as coal, oil, and wood.

DISCUSSION STARTER

How might Earth be different if it weren't tilted on its axis?

SCIENCE WORDS

community p. 50   fossil p. 40
consumer p. 54   genus p. 33
decomposer p. 54   habitat p. 50
ecosystem p. 50   kingdom p. 28
embryo p. 43   population p. 50
extinct p. 43   producer p. 54
food chain p. 56   species p. 33
food web p. 58   trait p. 28

USING SCIENCE WORDS

Number a paper from 1 to 10. Fill in 1 to 5 with words from the list above.

1. All the organisms in an ecosystem form a(n) __?__.

2. The first part of an organism's scientific name comes from its __?__ name.

3. The largest group into which an organism is classified is the __?__.

4. A characteristic of a living thing is known as a(n) __?__.

5. An organism that makes its own food is known as a(n) __?__.

6–10. Pick five words from the list above that were not used in 1 to 5, and use each in a sentence.

UNDERSTANDING SCIENCE IDEAS

11. Which classification group would have the most members? The least?

12. How can fossils help classify an extinct organism?

USING IDEAS AND SKILLS

13. **READING SKILL: COMPARE AND CONTRAST** Draw a diagram or chart that describes the relationships among producers, decomposers, and consumers.

14. **CLASSIFY** Classify the terms *habitat, population,* and *community* by completing this table. The table shows the living and non-living parts of an ecosystem. Give examples to illustrate each term.

Ecosystem
Living things include:
Nonliving things include:

15. **THINKING LIKE A SCIENTIST** How could scientific names be important in daily life?

PROBLEMS and PUZZLES

Sandy or Moist Would a houseplant grow best in sandy soil or moist potting soil? How could you test to find out? How could you be sure you are testing only the soil?

Field Test Look for plants growing in your neighborhood. Are some growing better than others? If so, try to determine why. You can take photographs to check your results.

SCIENCE WORDS

cell wall p. 14   habitat p. 50

cytoplasm p. 15   nucleus p. 15

ecosystem p. 50   organ p. 6

extinct p. 43   oxygen p. 4

fossil p. 40   species p. 33

genus p. 33   vacuole p. 15

USING SCIENCE WORDS

Number a paper from 1 to 10. Beside each number write the word or words that best completes the sentence.

1. Groups of tissues form a(n) __?__.

2. A holding bin for food, water, and wastes is called a(n) __?__.

3. The jellylike substance that fills a cell is called __?__.

4. The basic needs of most living things are food, water, a place to live, and __?__.

5. Evidence of an organism that lived in the past is called a(n) __?__.

6. If an organism is no longer alive on Earth, it is __?__.

7. A cell's control center is the __?__.

8. An organism's home is called its __?__.

9. An environment of living and non-living things is called a(n) __?__.

10. A group made up of two or more very similar species is called a(n) __?__.

UNDERSTANDING SCIENCE IDEAS

Write 11 to 15. For each number write the letter for the best answer. You may wish to use the hints provided.

11. The scientific naming system uses
    a. kingdom and phylum
    b. class and order
    c. genus and species
    d. family and kingdom
    (Hint: Read page 33, left column.)

12. Organisms that make food are
    a. consumers
    b. second consumers
    c. decomposers
    d. producers
    (Hint: Read page 54, right column.)

13. The main factor that makes one ecosystem differ from another is
    a. sunlight
    b. water
    c. soil
    d. people
    (Hint: Read page 52, left column.)

14. Humans would be considered
    a. producers
    b. consumers
    c. decomposers
    d. spoilers
    (Hint: Read pages 54–57.)

15. Which is an opinion supported by this unit?

   a. Humans can't control the destruction of Earth's ecosystems.

   b. Scientists have discovered most of the species on Earth.

   c. All parts of an ecosystem support one another.

   d. Only a few of the species that have ever lived are extinct.

(Hint: Read page 59, left column.)

USING IDEAS AND SKILLS

16. Discuss how an animal performs the five life functions.

17. Name three plant and three human organs. How are their jobs similar? Different?

18. How do people affect extinction? What do you think should be done about this?

19.  **CLASSIFY** Classify 20 things in your school as living or nonliving.

THINKING LIKE A SCIENTIST

20. **MAKE A MODEL** What materials would you use to make a model of *Tyrannosaurus rex*?

*inter*NET CONNECTION

For help in reviewing this unit, visit
www.mhschool.com/science

WRITING IN YOUR JOURNAL

GROWING UP

One of the basic life functions of living things is to grow and develop. You may not notice it, but you grow and develop every day. Make a list of things you can do now that you could not do when you were younger.

SEEING SCIENCE AROUND YOU

Have you ever traveled to somewhere very different from your home? How was it different? Was the weather different? Were there different animals and plants? If you lived there all the time, how would your life be different?

MAKING A DIFFERENCE

Every year in April, the world observes Earth Day. On Earth Day students do things to help keep Earth a healthy place to live. What could you and your friends do this Earth Day to help?

Design your own Experiment

Plants need water, sunlight, and air to survive, but which do they need most? Form a hypothesis. Design an experiment that tests which is most important.

PROBLEMS and PUZZLES

Organism Trading Cards

Make trading cards of your favorite organisms. On the front draw or paste a picture of the organism. On the back include information about its ecosystem, habitat, and genus and species name. Also include whether it is a producer, consumer, or decomposer. Use encyclopedias or other sources to find information. Challenge your friends to identify the organisms and to tell you anything else they may know about them. Trade them with your friends. It's a fun way to learn about organisms!

Ecosystem: my home
Habitat: under my blanket
Genus: Felis
Species: catus
Consumer

Brad's Birthday-Bread Baking Problem

THE PROBLEM
Brad's Birthday Bread won't rise. Brad's problem is that someone smeared dough on his recipe. He can't read whether to grow his yeast in cold, warm, or hot water. Yeast is a tiny fungus that makes bread rise. Yeast feeds on sugar and grows best at a certain temperature. Brad doesn't know what this temperature is.

THE PLAN
Write a hypothesis of how to make Brad's yeast grow. Think of a plan that will help you test your hypothesis.

TEST
Test Your Hypothesis Obtain yeast, sugar, and water. Your teacher will tell you how much of each ingredient to add. Then test your hypothesis. You can tell that the yeast is growing when it looks bubbly. At what water temperature does yeast grow best?

EVALUATE AND PUBLISH
Was your hypothesis correct? If not, how did you change it to find the best temperature for growing yeast?

Write a report that tells what you did.

REFERENCE SECTION

Temperature

1. The temperature is 77 degrees Fahrenheit.

2. That is the same as 25 degrees Celsius.

3. Water boils at 212 degrees Fahrenheit.

4. Water freezes at 0 degrees Celsius.

Length and Area

1. This classroom is 10 meters wide and 20 meters long.

2. That means the area is 200 square meters.

Mass and Weight

1. That baseball bat weighs 32 ounces.

2. 32 ounces is the same as 2 pounds.

3. The mass of the bat is 907 grams.

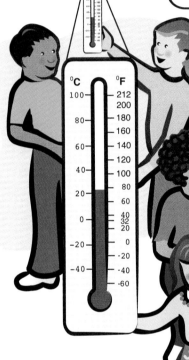

HANDBOOK

Volume of Fluids

1. This bottle of juice has a volume of 1 liter.

2. That is a little more than 1 quart.

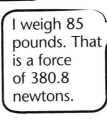

I weigh 85 pounds. That is a force of 380.8 newtons.

Weight/ Force

Rate

1. She can walk 20 meters in 5 seconds.

2. That means her speed is 4 meters per second.

Table of Measurements

SI (International System) of Units	English System of Units
Temperature Water freezes at 0 degrees Celsius (°C) and boils at 100°C.	**Temperature** Water freezes at 32 degrees Fahrenheit (°F) and boils at 212°F.
Length and Distance 10 millimeters (mm) = 1 centimeter (cm) 100 centimeters = 1 meter (m) 1,000 meters = 1 kilometer (km)	**Length and Distance** 12 inches (in.) = 1 foot (ft) 3 feet = 1 yard (yd) 5,280 feet = 1 mile (mi)
Volume 1 cubic centimeter (cm^3) = 1 milliliter (mL) 1,000 milliliters = 1 liter (L)	**Volume of Fluids** 8 fluid ounces (fl oz) = 1 cup (c) 2 cups = 1 pint (pt) 2 pints = 1 quart (qt) 4 quarts = 1 gallon (gal)
Mass 1,000 milligrams (mg) = 1 gram (g) 1,000 grams = 1 kilogram (kg)	**Weight** 16 ounces (oz) = 1 pound (lb) 2,000 pounds = 1 ton (T)
Area 1 square kilometer (km^2) = l km x l km 1 hectare = 10,000 square meters (m^2)	**Rate** mph = miles per hour
Rate m/s = meters per second km/h = kilometers per hour	
Force 1 newton (N) = 1 kg x m/s^2	

In the Classroom

The most important part of doing any experiment is doing it safely. You can be safe by paying attention to your teacher and doing your work carefully. Here are some other ways to stay safe while you do experiments.

Before the Experiment

- Read all of the directions. Make sure you understand them. When you see ▨, be sure to follow the safety rule.
- Listen to your teacher for special safety directions. If you don't understand something, ask for help.
- Wash your hands with soap and water before an activity.

During the Experiment

- Wear safety goggles when your teacher tells you to wear them and whenever you see ▨. Wear goggles when working with something that can fly into your eyes.
- Wear splash-proof goggles when working with liquids.
- Wear a safety apron if you work with anything messy or anything that might spill.

- If you spill something, wipe it up right away or ask your teacher for help.
- Tell your teacher if something breaks. If glass breaks do not clean it up yourself.
- Keep your hair and clothes away from open flames. Tie back long hair and roll up long sleeves.

- Be careful around a hot plate. Know when it is on and when it is off. Remember that the plate stays hot for a few minutes after you turn it off.
- Keep your hands dry around electrical equipment.
- Don't eat or drink anything during the experiment.

After the Experiment

- Put equipment back the way your teacher tells you.
- Dispose of things the way your teacher tells you.
- Clean up your work area and wash your hands with soap and water.

HANDBOOK

In the Field

- Always be accompanied by a trusted adult—like your teacher or a parent or guardian.
- Never touch animals or plants without the adult's approval. The animal might bite. The plant might be poison ivy or another dangerous plant.

Responsibility

Acting safely is one way to be responsible. You can also be responsible by treating animals, the environment, and each other with respect in the class and in the field.

Treat Living Things with Respect

- If you have animals in the classroom, keep their homes clean. Change the water in fish tanks and clean out cages.
- Feed classroom animals the right amounts of food.

- Give your classroom animals enough space.
- When you observe animals, don't hurt them or disturb their homes.
- Find a way to care for animals while school is on vacation.

Treat the Environment with Respect

- Do not pick flowers.
- Do not litter, including gum and food.
- If you see litter, ask your teacher if you can pick it up.

- Recycle materials used in experiments. Ask your teacher what materials can be recycled instead of thrown away. These might include plastics, aluminum, and newspapers.

Treat Each Other with Respect

- Use materials carefully around others so that people don't get hurt or get stains on their clothes.
- Be careful not to bump people when they are doing experiments. Do not disturb or damage their experiments.
- If you see that people are having trouble with an experiment, help them.

Use a Hand Lens

You use a hand lens to magnify an object, or make the object look larger. With a hand lens, you can see details that would be hard to see without the hand lens.

Magnify a Piece of Cereal

1. Place a piece of your favorite cereal on a flat surface. Look at the cereal carefully. Draw a picture of it.

2. Hold the hand lens so that it is just above the cereal. Look through the lens, and slowly move it away from the cereal. The cereal will look larger.

3. Keep moving the hand lens until the cereal begins to look blurry. Then move the lens a little closer to the cereal until you can see it clearly.

4. Draw a picture of the cereal as you see it through the hand lens. Fill in details that you did not see before.

5. Repeat this activity using objects you are studying in science. It might be a rock, some soil, a flower, a seed, or something else.

HANDBOOK

Use a Microscope

Hand lenses make objects look several times larger. A micro-scope, however, can magnify an object to look hundreds of times larger.

Examine Salt Grains

1. Place the microscope on a flat sur-face. Always carry a microscope with both hands. Hold the arm with one hand, and put your other hand beneath the base.
2. Look at the drawing to learn the different parts of the microscope.
3. Move the mirror so that it reflects light up toward the stage. Never point the mirror directly at the Sun or a bright light. Bright light can cause permanent eye damage.
4. Place a few grains of salt on the slide. Put the slide under the stage clips on the stage. Be sure that the salt grains are over the hole in the stage.
5. Look through the eyepiece. Turn the focusing knob slowly until the salt grains come into focus.
6. Draw what the grains look like through the microscope.
7. Look at other objects through the microscope. Try a piece of leaf, a strand of human hair, or a pencil mark.
8. Draw what each object looks like through the microscope. Do any of the objects look alike? If so, how? Are any of the objects alive? How do you know?

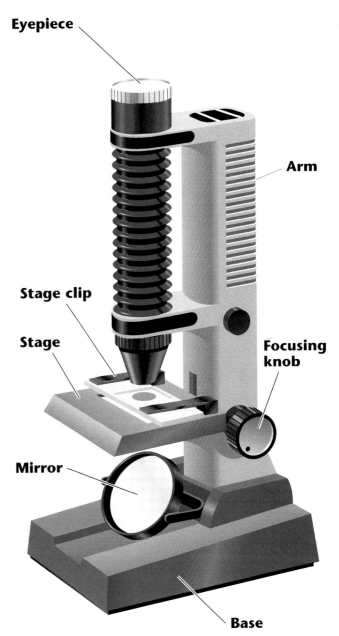

Eyepiece

Arm

Stage clip

Stage

Focusing knob

Mirror

Base

Use a Compass

You use a compass to find directions. A compass is a small, thin magnet that swings freely, like a spinner in a board game. One end of the magnet always points north. This end is the magnet's north pole. How does a compass work?

1. Place the compass on a surface that has no magnetic material such as steel. A wooden table or a sidewalk works well.
2. Find the magnet's north pole. The north pole is marked in some way, usually with a color or an arrowhead.
3. Notice the letters N, E, S, and W on the compass. These letters stand for the directions north, east, south, and west. When the magnet stops swinging, turn the compass so that the N lines up with the north pole of the magnet.
4. Face to the north. Then face to the east, to the south, and to the west.
5. Repeat this activity by holding the compass in your hand and then at different places indoors and outdoors.

Use a Compass to Study Shadows

A shadow is the shade that something makes when that thing blocks light. A shadow points away from the light that causes it. Find out how shadows change as the Sun moves across the sky.

1. Go outside on a sunny morning, and look at your shadow. Hold a compass flat in the palm of your hand. In which direction is your shadow pointing? In which direction is the Sun in the sky?
2. Go outside late in the afternoon with the compass. Now in which direction is your shadow pointing? In which direction is the Sun in the sky?

Use a Telescope

Have you ever seen the Moon near the horizon? A little while later, the Moon is higher in the sky. The Moon appears to move across the sky because Earth turns. Do stars appear to move across the sky, too? Make these observations on a clear night to find out.

Look at the Stars

1. Pick out a group of stars that you would be able to find again. The Big Dipper is a good choice. Choose a star in the star group.
2. Notice where the star is located compared to a treetop, a house roof, or some other point on land.
3. Find the same star an hour later. Notice that it appears to have moved in the sky. Predict how far the star will appear to move in another hour. Observe the star in an hour to check your prediction.

A telescope gathers light better than your eyes can. With a telescope you can see stars that you could not see with just your eyes.

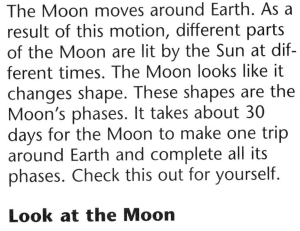

The Moon moves around Earth. As a result of this motion, different parts of the Moon are lit by the Sun at different times. The Moon looks like it changes shape. These shapes are the Moon's phases. It takes about 30 days for the Moon to make one trip around Earth and complete all its phases. Check this out for yourself.

Look at the Moon

1. Make a calendar that shows the next 30 days.
2. Each day draw in the Moon's shape in the calendar box for that day. How many days does it take to come back to the same shape?

Use a Camera, Tape Recorder, Map, and Compass

Camera

You can use a camera to record what you observe in nature. Keep these tips in mind.

1. Hold the camera steady. Gently press the button so that you do not jerk the camera.
2. Try to take pictures with the Sun at your back. Then your pictures will be bright and clear.
3. Don't get too close to the subject. Without a special lens, the picture could turn out blurry.
4. Be patient. If you are taking a picture of an animal, you may have to wait for the animal to appear.

Tape Recorder

You can record observations on a tape recorder. This is sometimes better than writing notes because a tape recorder can record your observations at the exact time you are making them. Later you can listen to the tape and write down your observations.

Map and Compass

When you are busy observing nature, it might be easy to get lost. You can use a map of the area and a compass to find your way. Here are some tips.

1. Lightly mark on the map your starting place. It might be the place where the bus parked.
2. Always know where you are on the map compared to your starting place. Watch for landmarks on the map, such as a river, a pond, trails, or buildings.
3. Use the map and compass to find special places to observe, such as a pond. Look at the map to see which direction the place is from you. Hold the compass to see where that direction is.
4. Use your map and compass with a friend.

Length

MATH LINK

Find Length with a Ruler

1. Look at this section of a ruler. Each centimeter is divided into 10 millimeters. How long is the paper clip?

2. The length of the paper clip is 3 centimeters plus 2 millimeters. You can write this length as 3.2 centimeters.

3. Place the ruler on your desk. Lay a pencil against the ruler so that one end of the pencil lines up with the left edge of the ruler. Record the length of the pencil.

4. Trade your pencil with a classmate. Measure and record the length of each other's pencils. Compare your answers.

Measuring Area

Area is the amount of surface something covers. To find the area of a rectangle, multiply the rectangle's length by its width. For example, the rectangle here is 3 centimeters long and 2 centimeters wide. Its area is 3 cm x 2 cm = 6 square centimeters. You write the area as 6 cm².

1. Find the area of your science book. Measure the book's length to the nearest centimeter. Measure its width.

2. Multiply the book's length by its width. Remember to put the answer in cm².

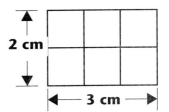

2 cm

3 cm

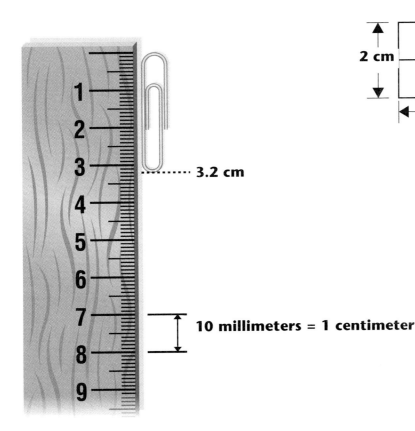

3.2 cm

10 millimeters = 1 centimeter

Time

You use timing devices to measure how long something takes to happen. Some timing devices you use in science are a clock with a second hand and a stopwatch. Which one is more accurate?

Comparing a Clock and a Stopwatch

1. Look at a clock with a second hand. The second hand is the hand that you can see moving. It measures seconds.

2. Get an egg timer with falling sand or some device like a windup toy that runs down after a certain length of time. When the second hand of the clock points to 12, tell your partner to start the egg timer. Watch the clock while the sand in the egg timer is falling.

3. When the sand stops falling, count how many seconds it took. Record this measurement. Repeat the activity, and compare the two measurements.

4. Switch roles with your partner.

5. Look at a stopwatch. Click the button on the top right. This starts the time. Click the button again. This stops the time. Click the button on the top left. This sets the stopwatch back to zero. Notice that the stopwatch tells time in hours, minutes, seconds, and hundredths of a second.

6. Repeat the activity in steps 1–3, but use the stopwatch instead of a clock. Make sure the stopwatch is set to zero. Click the top right button to start timing.

Click the button again when the sand stops falling. Make sure you and your partner time the sand twice.

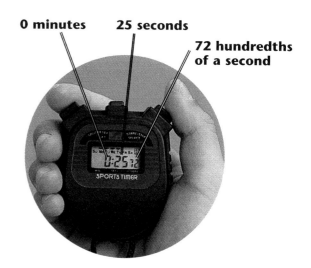

0 minutes   25 seconds
72 hundredths of a second

More About Time

1. Use the stopwatch to time how long it takes an ice cube to melt under cold running water. How long does an ice cube take to melt under warm running water?

2. Match each of these times with the action you think took that amount of time.

0.00.14:55	0.24.39:45	2.10.23:00
a.	**b.**	**c.**

1. A Little League baseball game

2. Saying the Pledge of Allegiance

3. Recess

Volume

Have you ever used a measuring cup? Measuring cups measure the volume of liquids. Volume is the amount of space something takes up. To bake a cake, you might measure the volume of water, vegetable oil, or melted butter. In science you use special measuring cups called beakers and graduated cylinders. These containers are marked in milliliters (mL).

Measure the Volume of a Liquid

1. Look at the beaker and at the graduated cylinder. The beaker has marks for each 25 mL up to 200 mL. The graduated cylinder has marks for each 1 mL up to 100 mL.

2. The surface of the water in the graduated cylinder curves up at the sides. You measure the volume by reading the height of the water at the flat part. What is the volume of water in the graduated cylinder? How much water is in the beaker? They both contain 75 mL of water.

3. Pour 50 mL of water from a pitcher into a graduated cylinder. The water should be at the 50-mL mark on the graduated cylinder. If you go over the mark, pour a little water back into the pitcher.

4. Pour the 50 mL of water into a beaker.

5. Repeat steps 3 and 4 using 30 mL, 45 mL, and 25 mL of water.

6. Measure the volume of water you have in the beaker. Do you have about the same amount of water as your classmates?

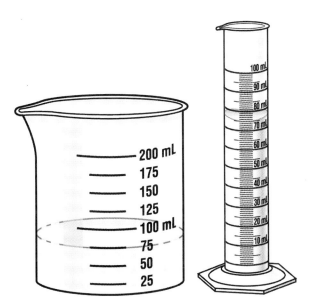

MATH LINK

HANDBOOK

Mass

Mass is the amount of matter an object has. You use a balance to measure mass. To find the mass of an object, you balance it with objects whose masses you know. Let's find the mass of a box of crayons.

Measure the Mass of a Box of Crayons

1. Place the balance on a flat, level surface. Check that the two pans are empty and clean.
2. Make sure the empty pans are balanced with each other. The pointer should point to the middle mark. If it does not, move the slider a little to the right or left to balance the pans.

3. Gently place a box of crayons on the left pan. This pan will drop lower.
4. Add masses to the right pan until the pans are balanced.
5. Add the numbers on the masses that are in the right pan. The total is the mass of the box of crayons, in grams. Record this number. After the number, write a *g* for "grams."

Predict the Mass of More Crayons

1. Leave the box of crayons and the masses on the balance.
2. Get two more crayons. If you put them in the pan with the box of crayons, what do you think the mass of all the crayons will be? Write down what you predict the total mass will be.
3. Check your prediction. Gently place the two crayons in the left pan. Add masses to the right pan until the pans are balanced.
4. Add the numbers on the masses as you did before. Record this number. How close is it to your prediction?

More About Mass

What was the mass of all your crayons? It was probably less than 100 grams. What would happen if you replaced the crayons with a pineapple? You may not have enough masses to balance the pineapple. It has a mass of about 1,000 grams. That's the same as 1 kilogram because *kilo* means "1,000."

1. How many kilograms do all these masses add up to?

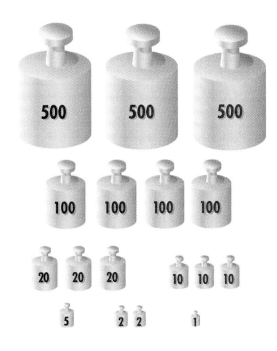

2. Which of these objects have a mass greater than 1 kilogram?
    a. large dog
    b. robin
    c. desktop computer
    d. calculator
    e. whole watermelon

Weight/Force

You use a spring scale to measure weight. An object has weight because the force of gravity pulls down on the object. Therefore, weight is a force. Like all forces weight is measured in newtons (N).

Measure the Weight of an Object

1. Look at your spring scale to see how many newtons it measures. See how the measurements are divided. The spring scale shown here measures up to 10 N. It has a mark for every 1 N.

2. Hold the spring scale by the top loop. Put the object to be measured on the bottom hook. If the object will not stay on the hook, place it in a net bag. Then hang the bag from the hook.

3. Let go of the object slowly. It will pull down on a spring inside the scale. The spring is connected to a pointer. The pointer on the spring scale shown here is a small arrow.

4. Wait for the pointer to stop moving. Read the number of newtons next to the pointer. This is the object's weight. The mug in the picture weighs 3 N.

More About Spring Scales

You probably weigh yourself by standing on a bathroom scale. This is a spring scale. The force of your body stretches a spring inside the scale. The dial on the scale is probably marked in pounds—the English unit of weight. One pound is equal to about 4.5 newtons.

Here are some spring scales you may have seen.

Temperature

Temperature is how hot or cold something is. You use a thermometer to measure temperature. A thermometer is made of a thin tube with colored liquid inside. When the liquid gets warmer, it expands and moves up the tube. When the liquid gets cooler, it contracts and moves down the tube. You may have seen most temperatures measured in degrees Fahrenheit (°F). Scientists measure temperature in degrees Celsius (°C).

Read a Thermometer

1. Look at the thermometer shown here. It has two scales—a Fahrenheit scale and a Celsius scale. Every 20 degrees on each scale has a number.

2. What is the temperature shown on the thermometer? At what temperature does water freeze? Give your answers in °F and in °C.

How Is Temperature Measured?

1. Fill a large beaker about one-half full of cool water. Find the temperature of the water by holding a thermometer in the water. Do not let the bulb at the bottom of the thermometer touch the sides or bottom of the beaker.

2. Keep the thermometer in the water until the liquid in the tube stops moving—about a minute. Read and record the temperature on the Celsius scale.

3. Fill another large beaker one-half full of warm water from a faucet. Be careful not to burn yourself by using hot water.

4. Find and record the temperature of the warm water just as you did in steps 1 and 2.

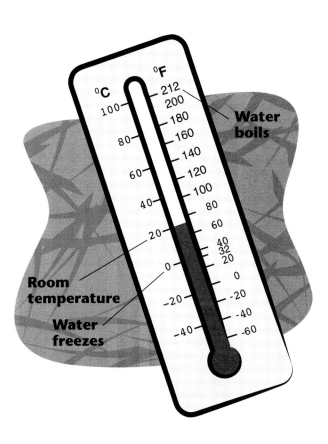

Weather

What was the weather like yesterday? What is it like today? The weather changes from day to day. You can observe different parts of the weather to find out how it changes.

Measure Temperature

1. Use a thermometer to find the air temperature outside. Look at page R17 to review thermometers.
2. Hold a thermometer outside for two minutes. Then read and record the temperature.
3. Take the temperature at the same time each day for a week. Record it in a chart.

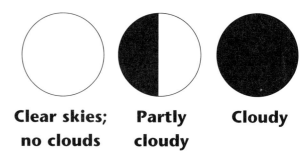

Clear skies; no clouds   **Partly cloudy**   **Cloudy**

2. Record in your chart if it is raining or snowing.
3. At the end of the week, how has the weather changed from day to day?

Observe Wind Speed and Direction

1. Observe how the wind is affecting things around you. Look at a flag or the branches of a tree. How hard is the wind blowing the flag or branches? Observe for about five minutes. Write down your observations.
2. Hold a compass to see which direction the wind is coming from. Write down this direction.
3. Observe the wind each day for a week. Record your observations in your chart.

Observe Clouds, Rain, and Snow

1. Observe how much of the sky is covered by clouds. Use these symbols to record the cloud cover in your chart each day.

MONDAY	TUESDAY	WEDNESDAY
25ºC Strong winds from south ● Rain	23ºC Light wind	

Systems

What do a toy car, a tomato plant, and a yo-yo have in common? They are all systems. A system is a set of parts that work together to form a whole. Look at the three systems below. Think of how each part helps the system work.

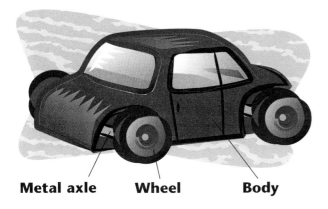

Metal axle   **Wheel**   **Body**

This system has three main parts—the body, the axles, and the wheels. Would the system work well if the axles could not turn?

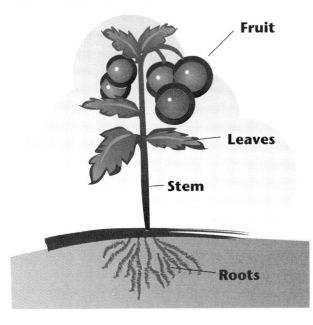

Fruit

Leaves

Stem

Roots

In this system roots take in water, and leaves make food. The stem carries water and food to different parts of the plant. What would happen if you cut off all the leaves?

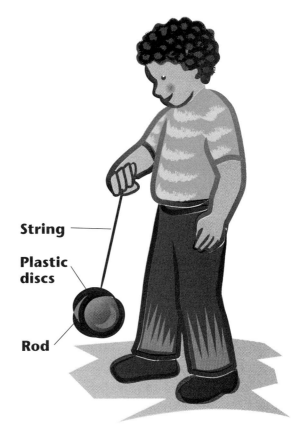

String

Plastic discs

Rod

Even simple things can be systems. How do all the parts of the yo-yo work together to make the toy go up and down?

Look for some other systems at school, at home, and outside. Remember to look for things that are made of parts. List the parts. Then describe how you think each part helps the system work.

Make Graphs to Organize Data

When you do an experiment in science, you collect information. To find out what your information means, you can organize it into graphs. There are many kinds of graphs.

Bar Graphs

A bar graph uses bars to show information. For example, suppose you are growing a plant. Every week you measure how high the plant has grown. Here is what you find.

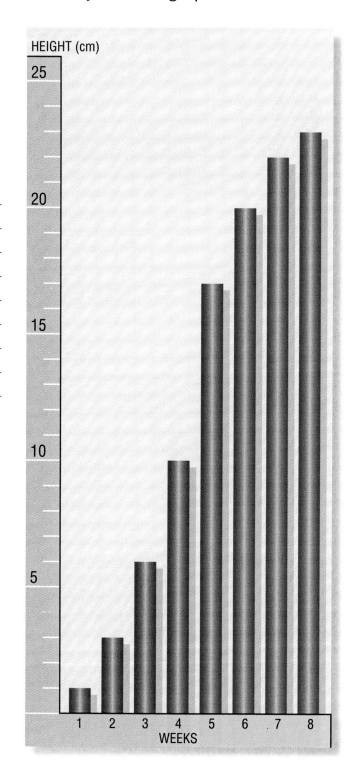

Week	Height (cm)
1	1
2	3
3	6
4	10
5	17
6	20
7	22
8	23

The bar graph at right organizes the measurements you collected so that you can easily compare them.

1. Look at the bar for week 2. Put your finger at the top of the bar. Move your finger straight over to the left to find how many centimeters the plant grew by the end of week 2.

2. Between which two weeks did the plant grow most?

3. When did plant growth begin to level off?

Pictographs

A pictograph uses symbols, or pictures, to show information. What if you collect information about how much water your family uses each day? Here is what you find.

Activity	Water Used Each Day (L)
Drinking	10
Showering	180
Bathing	240
Brushing teeth	80
Washing dishes	140
Washing hands	30
Washing clothes	280
Flushing toilet	90

You can organize this information into the pictograph shown here. The pictograph has to explain what the symbol on the graph means. In this case each bottle means 20 liters of water. A half bottle means half of 20, or 10 liters of water.

1. Which activity uses the most water?
2. Which activity uses the least water?

Line Graphs

A line graph shows information by connecting dots plotted on the graph.

It shows change over time. For example, what if you measure the temperature out of doors every hour starting at 6 A.M.? Here is what you find.

Time	Temperature (°C)
6 A.M.	10
7 A.M.	12
8 A.M.	14
9 A.M.	16
10 A.M.	18
11 A.M.	20

You can organize this information into a line graph. Follow these steps.

1. Make a scale along the bottom and side of the graph. The scales should include all the numbers in the chart. Label the scales.
2. Plot points on the graph. For example, place your finger at the "6 A.M." on the bottom line. Place a finger from your other hand on the "10" on the left line. Move your "6 A.M." finger up and your "10" finger to the right until they meet, and make a pencil point. Plot the other points in this way.
3. Connect the points with a line.

A Family's Daily Use of Water

Make Maps to Show Information

Locate Places

A map is a drawing that shows an area from above. Most maps have numbers and letters along the top and side. They help you find places easily. For example, what if you wanted to find the library on the map below. It is located at D7. Place a finger on the letter D along the side of the map and another finger on the number 7 at the top. Then move your fingers straight across and down the map until they meet. The library is located where D and 7 meet, or very nearby.

1. What building is located at G3?
2. The hospital is located three blocks south and three blocks east of the library. What is its number and letter?
3. Make a map of an area in your community. It might be a park or the area between your home and school. Include numbers and letters along the top and side. Use a compass to find north, and mark north on your map. Exchange maps with classmates.

Idea Maps

The map below left shows how places are connected to each other. Idea maps, on the other hand, show how ideas are connected to each other. Idea maps help you organize information about a topic.

Look at the idea map below. It connects ideas about water. This map shows that Earth's water is either fresh water or salt water. The map also shows four sources of fresh water. You can see that there is no connection between "rivers" and "salt water" on the map. This reminds you that salt water does not flow in rivers.

Make an idea map about a topic you are learning in science. Your map can include words, phrases, or even sentences. Arrange your map in a way that makes sense to you and helps you understand the ideas.

Make Tables and Charts to Organize Data

Tables help you organize data during experiments. Most tables have columns that run up and down, and rows that run across. The columns and rows have headings that tell you what kind of data goes in each part of the table.

A Sample Table

What if you are going to do an experiment to find out how long different kinds of seeds take to sprout? Before you begin the experiment, you should set up your table. Follow these steps.

1. In this experiment you will plant 20 radish seeds, 20 bean seeds, and 20 corn seeds. Your table must show how many of each kind of seed sprouted on days 1, 2, 3, 4, and 5.
2. Make your table with columns, rows, and headings. You might use a computer. Some computer programs let you build a table with just the click of a mouse. You can delete or add columns and rows if you need to.
3. Give your table a title. Your table could look like the one here.

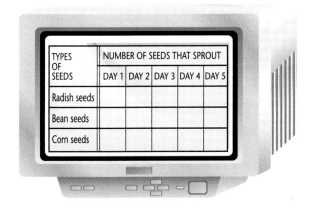

TYPES OF SEEDS	NUMBER OF SEEDS THAT SPROUT				
	DAY 1	DAY 2	DAY 3	DAY 4	DAY 5
Radish seeds					
Bean seeds					
Corn seeds					

Make a Table

Now what if you are going to do an experiment to find out how temperature affects the sprouting of seeds? You will plant 20 bean seeds in each of two trays. You will keep each tray at a different temperature, as shown below, and observe the trays for seven days. Make a table that you can use for this experiment. You can use the table to record, examine, and evaluate the information of this experiment.

Make a Chart

A chart is simply a table with pictures as well as words to label the rows or columns. Make a chart that shows the information of the above experiment.

Computer

A computer has many uses. The Internet connects your computer to many other computers around the world, so you can collect all kinds of information. You can use a computer to show this information and write reports. Best of all you can use a computer to explore, discover, and learn.

You can also get information from CD-ROMs. They are computer disks that can hold large amounts of information. You can fit a whole encyclopedia on one CD-ROM.

Use Computers for a Project

Here is how one group of students uses computers as they work on a weather project.

1. The students use instruments to measure temperature, wind speed, wind direction, and other parts of the weather. They input this information, or data, into the computer. The students keep the data in a table. This helps them compare the data from one day to the next.

2. The teacher finds out that another group of students in a town 200 kilometers to the west is also doing a weather project. The two groups use the Internet to talk to each other and share data. When a storm happens in the town to the west, that group tells the other group that it's coming its way.

email: It's going to storm here. The sky is turning dark gray. The winds are sometimes 65 km per hour from the northwest.

4. Meanwhile some students go to the library to gather more information from a CD-ROM disk. The CD-ROM has an encyclopedia that includes movie clips with sound. The clips give examples of different kinds of storms.

5. The students have kept all their information in a folder called Weather Project. Now they use that information to write a report about the weather. On the computer they can move paragraphs, add words, take out words, put in diagrams, and draw their own weather maps. Then they print the report in color.

3. The students want to find out more. They decide to stay on the Internet and send questions to a local TV weather forecaster. She has a Web site and answers questions from students every day.

6. Use the information on these two pages to plan your own investigation. You can study the weather. Use a computer, Internet, CD-ROM, or any other technological device.

Calculator

Sometimes after you make measurements, you have to multiply or divide your measurements to get other information. A calculator helps you multiply and divide, especially if the numbers have decimal points.

Multiply Decimals

What if you are measuring the width of your classroom? You discover that the floor is covered with tiles and the room is exactly 32 tiles wide. You measure a tile, and it is 22.7 centimeters wide. To find the width of the room, you can multiply 32 by 22.7. You can use your calculator.

1. Make sure the calculator is on. Press the **ON** key.
2. Press **3** and **2**.
3. Press **×**.
4. Press **2**, **2**, **.**, and **7**.
5. Press **=**. Your total should be 726.4. That is how wide the room is in centimeters.

Divide Decimals

Now what if you wanted to find out how many desks placed side by side would be needed to reach across the room? You measure one desk, and it is 60 centimeters wide. To find the number of desks needed, divide 726.4 by 60.

1. Turn the calculator on.
2. Press **7**, **2**, **6**, **.**, and **4**.
3. Press **÷**.
4. Press **6** and **0**.
5. Press **=**. Your total should be about 12.1. This means you can fit 12 desks across the room with a little space left over.

What if the room was 35 tiles wide? How wide would the room be? How many desks would fit across it?

GLOSSARY

This Glossary will help you to pronounce and understand the meanings of the Science Words introduced in this book. The page number at the end of the definition tells where the word appears.

A

abuse (*v.*, ə būz′; *n.*, ə būs′) To use legal drugs in an unsafe way on purpose or to use illegal drugs. (p. 474)

adaptation (ad′əp tā′shən) A special trait that helps an organism survive. (p. 276)

addictive (ə dik′tiv) Causing dependence, or a strong need to have a particular substance. (p. 460)

alcohol (al′kə hôl′) A drug found in beer, wine, liquor, and even some medications. (p. 458)

allergy (al′ər jē) A sensitivity to a substance that can cause a rash, fever, or trouble breathing. (p. 471)

alloy (al′oi) A mixture of two or more metals. (p. 96)

alternating current (ôl′tər nā ting kûr′ənt) Current that flows in a circuit first in one direction, then in the opposite direction. (p. 342)

amber (am′bər) Hardened tree sap, yellow to brown in color, often a source of insect fossils. (p. 164)

amphibian (am fib′ē ən) A cold-blooded vertebrate that spends part of its life in water and part of its life on land. (p. 239)

antibiotic (an′tē bī ot′ik) A type of medicine that kills bacteria or stops them from growing. (p. 470)

area (âr′ē ə) The number of unit squares that fit inside a surface. (p. 81)

arthropod (är′thrə pod′) An invertebrate with jointed legs and a body that is divided into sections. (p. 227)

asexual reproduction (a sek′shü əl rē′prə duk′shən) Producing offspring with only one parent. (p. 268)

atmosphere (at′məs fîr′) Gases that surround Earth. (p. 372)

atom (at′əm) The smallest particle of an element that has all the properties of that element. (p. 88)

B

bacteria (bak tîr′ē ə) *pl., sing.* **bacterium** (bak tîr′ē əm) One-celled organisms that have cell walls but no nuclei. (p. 19)

balance (bal′əns) An instrument used to measure mass. (p. 70)

biceps (bī′seps) A muscle in the upper arm that bends the arm by contracting. (p. 446)

bilateral symmetry (bī lat′ər əl sim′ə trē) A form of symmetry in which an animal has only two sides, which are mirror images. (p. 215)

bladder (blad′ər) The body structure that stores urine until it is removed from the body. (p. 254)

PRONUNCIATION KEY

a	at	e	end	o	hot	u	up	hw	white	ə	about
ā	ape	ē	me	ō	old	ū	use	ng	song		taken
ä	far	i	it	ô	fork	ü	rule	th	thin		pencil
âr	care	ī	ice	oi	oil	u̇	pull	t̲h̲	this		lemon
		îr	pierce	ou	out	ûr	turn	zh	measure		circus

′ = *primary accent; shows which syllable takes the main stress, such as* **kil** *in* **kilogram** (kil′ə gram′)
′ = *secondary accent; shows which syllables take lighter stresses, such as* **gram** *in* **kilogram**

budding (bud'ing) A form of asexual reproduction in simple invertebrates where a bud forms on the adult's body and slowly develops into a new animal before breaking off. (p. 268)

buoyancy (boi'ən sē) The upward force of a liquid or gas. (p. 69)

C

caffeine (ka fēn') A stimulant found in tea, coffee, and many soft drinks. (p. 472)

camouflage (kam'ə fläzh') An adaptation by which an animal can hide by blending in with its surroundings. (p. 276)

carbon monoxide (kär'bən mon ok'sīd) A poisonous gas given off by burning tobacco. (p. 462)

cardiac muscle (kär'dē ak' mus'əl) The type of muscle that makes up the heart. (p. 448)

carnivore (kär'nə vôr') A consumer that eats only animals. (p. 56)

cartilage (kär'tə lij) A flexible tissue that covers the ends of some bones; found in the nose and ears. (p. 439)

cartilaginous (kär'tə laj'ə nəs) Said of a fish with a skeleton made of cartilage. (p. 237)

cast (kast) A fossil formed or shaped within a mold. (p. 163)

cell (sel) The smallest unit of living matter. (p. 5)

cell membrane (sel mem'brān) An animal cell's thin outer covering. It is found beneath the cell wall in plants. (p. 15)

cell wall (sel wôl) A thick, stiff structure that protects and supports a plant cell. (p. 14)

chemical change (kem'i kəl chānj) A change that produces new matter with different properties from the original matter. *See* **physical change**. (p. 104)

chitin (kī'tin) A light but tough material that makes up the exoskeletons of certain invertebrates. (p. 228)

chlorophyll (klôr'ə fil') A material (usually green) found in plant cells that makes food for the plant when sunlight strikes it. (p. 5)

chloroplast (klôr'ə plast') A plant cell's food factory. Chloroplasts contain a substance (usually green) that uses the Sun's energy to make food. (p. 14)

chromosome (krō'mə sōm') One of the threadlike structures inside a cell nucleus that determine an organism's traits. (p. 16)

circuit (sûr'kit) A complete path that electricity can move through. (p. 304)

circuit breaker (sûr'kit brā'kər) A reusable switch that protects circuits from dangerously high currents. (p. 322)

circulatory system (sûr'kyə lə tôr'ē sis'təm) The organ system that moves blood through the body. (p. 252)

class (klas) A smaller group within a phylum, such as all those animals that produce milk for their young. Classes are made up of smaller groups called *orders*. (p. 30)

clone (klōn) An exact copy of its parent formed by asexual reproduction. (p. 268)

closed circuit (klōzd sûr'kit) A clear and complete path that electricity can flow through. (p. 305)

cloud (kloud) Tiny drops of condensed water that gather in the atmosphere. (p. 385)

cnidarian (nī dâr'ē ən) An invertebrate with poison stingers on tentacles. (p. 223)

cocaine (kō kān') An illegal stimulant made from the leaves of the coca plant. (p. 473)

cold-blooded (kōld'blud'id) Said of an animal that cannot control its body temperature. (p. 236)

community (kə mū'ni tē) The living part of an ecosystem. (p. 50)

compound (kom'pound) A substance made when two or more elements are joined and lose their own properties. (p. 94)

compound machine (kom′pound mə shēn′) A combination of two or more machines. (p. 139)

condensation (kon′den sā′shən) When water particles change from a gas to a liquid. (p. 385)

conduction (kən duk′shən) The transfer of energy caused by one particle of matter hitting into another. (p. 118)

conductor (kən duk′tər) 1. A material that transfers heat well. (p. 116) 2. Said of a material through which electricity flows easily. (p. 295)

consumer (kən sü′mər) Any organism that eats the food producers make. (p. 54)

continental glacier (kon′tə nen′təl glā′shər) A glacier covering large sections of land in Earth's polar regions. (p. 177)

contract (v., kən trakt′) To decrease in size, or shrink, as most matter does when it cools. (p. 120)

convection (kən′vek′shən) The transfer of energy by the flow of liquids or gases, such as water boiling in a pot or warm air rising in a room. (p. 118)

crack (krak) A very harmful form of cocaine. (p. 473)

crust (krust) Solid rock that makes up Earth's outermost layer. (p. 202)

crystal (kris′təl) The clear and shiny particle of frozen water that makes up a snowflake. (p. 390)

current (kûr′ənt) An ocean movement; a large stream of water that flows in the ocean. (p. 396)

current electricity (kûr′ənt i lek tris′i tē) A moving electrical charge. (p. 304)

cytoplasm (sī′tə plaz′əm) A jellylike substance that fills a cell. (p. 15)

D

decomposer (dē′kəm pō′zər) An organism that breaks down wastes and the remains of other organisms. (p. 54)

deep ocean current (dēp ō′shən kûr′ənt) A stream of water that flows more than 200 meters (650 feet) beneath the sea. (p. 396)

density (den′si tē) The amount of matter in a given space. In scientific terms density is the mass per unit of volume. (p. 84)

dependence (di pen′dəns) A strong need or desire for a medicine or drug. (p. 471)

depressant (di pres′ənt) A drug that slows down the activity of the body. (p. 459)

diaphragm (dī′ə fram′) A muscle below the lungs. When relaxed the diaphragm pushes up. Air leaves the lungs. When the diaphragm flattens and pulls down, the lungs fill with air. (p. 253)

digestive system (di jes′tiv sis′təm) The organ system that breaks down food for fuel. (p. 255)

direct current (di rekt′ kûr′ənt) Current that flows in one direction through a circuit. (p. 342)

discharge (v., dis chärj′; n., dis′chärj) When a buildup of electrical charge empties into something. (p. 295)

drought (drout) A long period of time with little or no precipitation. (p. 412)

drug (drug) A substance other than food that changes the way a person feels, thinks, and acts. (p. 458)

drumlin (drum′lin) An oval mound of glacial till. (p. 177)

PRONUNCIATION KEY

a at; ā ape; ä far; âr care; e end; ē me; i it; ī ice; îr pierce; o hot; ō old; ô fork; oi oil; ou out; u up; ū use; ü rule; u̇ pull; ûr turn; hw white; ng song; th thin; <u>th</u> this; zh measure; ə about, taken, pencil, lemon, circus

GLOSSARY

dry cell (drī sel) A battery that changes chemical energy into electrical energy. It is made of a carbon rod and a moist chemical paste. (p. 306)

E

earthquake (ûrth'kwāk') Movement or vibration in the rocks that make up Earth's crust. (p. 198)

echinoderm (i kī'nə dûrm') A spiny-skinned invertebrate. (p. 226)

ecology (ē kol'ə jē) The study of how living and nonliving things interact. (p. 50)

ecosystem (ek'ō sis'təm) The living and nonliving things in an environment and all their interactions. (p. 50)

effort force (ef'ərt fôrs) The force applied to a machine. (p. 132)

egg (eg) The female sex cell. (p. 269)

electrical charge (i lek'tri kəl chärj) The positive or negative property of the particles that make up matter. (p. 292)

electricity (i lek tris'i tē) The energy caused by the flow of particles with negative electrical charges. (p. 292)

electrode (i lek'trōd) The negative or positive terminal of a wet cell. (p. 344)

electromagnet (i lek'trō mag'nit) A temporary magnet created when current flows through wire wrapped in coils around an iron bar. (p. 333)

element (el'ə mənt) A substance that is made up of only one type of matter. (p. 90)

embryo (em'brē ō') A developing organism that results from fertilization; an undeveloped animal or plant. (pp. 43, 269)

endoskeleton (en'dō skel'i tən) An internal supporting structure. (p. 226)

energy (en'ər jē) The ability to do work. (p. 129)

energy transformation (en'ər jē trans'fər mā'shən) A change of energy from one form to another. (p. 354)

erosion (i rō'zhən) The wearing away of rocks and rock materials, as when glaciers leave distinctive features on Earth's surface. (p. 155)

erratic (i rat'ik) An isolated boulder left behind by a glacier. (p. 179)

evaporation (i vap'ə rā'shən) The change of a liquid to a gas. (pp. 93, 384)

evolution (ev'ə lü'shən) The change in living things over time. (p. 40)

excretory system (ek'skri tôr'ē sis'təm) The organ system that removes liquid wastes. (p. 254)

exoskeleton (ek'sō skel'i tən) A hard covering that protects the body of certain invertebrates. (p. 227)

expand (ek spand') To swell or get larger, as most matter does when it is heated. (p. 120)

expiration date (ek'spə rā'shən dāt) The date on a medicine label after which the medicine should not be used. (p. 470)

extinct (ek stingkt') Said of an organism no longer alive on Earth. (p. 43)

F

family (fam'ə lē) A smaller group of organisms within a class. Families are made up of still smaller groups of very similar organisms called *genuses*. (p. 30)

fault (fôlt) A break in Earth's outer layer caused by the movement of rocks. (p. 200)

fertilization (fûr'tə lə zā'shən) Occurs during sexual reproduction when an egg and a sperm join. (p. 269)

fertilizer (fûr′tə lī′zər) Chemicals or animal waste used to treat the soil so that plants grow stronger. (p. 423)

filter (fil′tər) A tool used to separate things by size. It works by means of an interwoven material that retains the bigger pieces but allows smaller pieces to fall through the holes of the filter. (p. 93)

filtration (fil trā′shən) The passing of a liquid through materials that remove solid impurities. (p. 424)

fixed pulley (fikst pul′ē) A pulley that does not increase the effort force needed to move an object but does change the direction of that force. The pulley wheel is attached to one place so that the object moves, not the wheel. *See* **pulley**. (p. 134)

food chain (füd chān) The set of steps in which organisms get the food they need to survive. (p. 48)

food web (füd web) The pattern that shows how food chains are related. (p. 48)

force (fôrs) The push or pull needed to make an object move. (p. 128)

fossil (fos′əl) Any evidence of an organism that lived in the past. (pp. 40, 156)

fracture (frak′chər) A break or crack in a bone. (p. 439)

freeze (frēz) When moving particles in water slow down, lose heat, and change from a liquid to a solid. (p. 387)

fungi (fun′jī) *pl., sing.* **fungus** (fung′gəs) One- or many-celled organisms that lack true roots, stems, and leaves, and absorb food from dead organisms. (p. 19)

fuse (fūz) A device that melts to keep too much electric current from flowing through wires. Once melted a fuse cannot be reused. (p. 322)

G

gas (gas) A form of matter that does not take up a definite amount of space and has no definite shape. (p. 71)

gears (gîrz) Wheels with teeth that transfer motion and force from one source to another. (pp. 138, 358)

generator (jen′ər rā′tər) A device that creates alternating current by spinning an electric coil between the poles of a powerful magnet. (p. 343)

genus (jē′nəs) A group made up of two or more very similar species, like dogs and wolves. (p. 33)

geologist (jē ol′ə jist) A scientist who studies the physical properties of rocks to tell how the rocks may have formed. (p. 148)

gizzard (giz′ərd) A muscular organ in birds that breaks down food by grinding it with stored pebbles. (p. 255)

glacial till (glā′shəl til) An unsorted mixture of rock materials deposited as a glacier melts. (p. 177)

glacier (glā′shər) A large mass of ice and snow that moves over land. (pp. 176, 373)

grounded (ground′əd) Said of an electric charge that flows into the ground, or surface of Earth. (p. 297)

groundwater (ground wô′tər) Water stored in the cracks of underground rocks. (p. 374)

H

habitat (hab′i tat′) The home of an organism. (p. 50)

heat (hēt) The movement of energy from warmer to cooler objects. (p. 116)

PRONUNCIATION KEY

a at; ā ape; ä far; âr care; e end; ē me; i it; ī ice; îr pierce; o hot; ō old; ô fork; oi oil; ou out; u up; ū use; ü rule; u̇ pull; ûr turn; hw white; ng song; th thin; th this; zh measure; ə about, taken, pencil, lemon, circus

herbivore (hər′ bə vôr′) A consumer that eats only plants. (p. 56)

heredity (hə red′i tē) The passing of traits from parent to offspring. (p. 270)

hibernate (hī′bər nāt′) An instinct that causes some animals to sleep through the winter; all body processes slow down, and body temperature can drop to a few degrees above freezing. (p. 280)

horizon (hə rī′zən) A layer of soil differing from the layers above and below it. (p. 187)

humus (hū′məs) Leftover decomposed plant and animal matter in the soil. (p. 186)

I

ice cap (īs kap) A thick sheet of ice covering a large area of land. (p. 373)

igneous rock (ig′nē əs rok) "Fire-made" rock formed from melted rock material. (p. 151)

immovable joint (i mü′və bəl joint) A place where bones fit together too tightly to move. (p. 438)

imprint (n., im′print′) A fossil created by a print or impression. (p. 162)

inclined plane (in klīnd′ plān) A straight, slanted surface that is not moved when it is used. (p. 136)

inherited behavior (in her′i təd bi hāv′yər) A behavior that is inborn, not learned. (p. 280)

inner core (in′ər kôr) A sphere of solid material at Earth's center. (p. 202)

instinct (in′stingkt′) A pattern of behavior that requires no thinking because it is programmed into an animal's brain. (p. 280)

insulator (in′sə lā′tər) 1. A material that does not transfer heat very well. (p. 116) 2. Said of a material through which electricity does not flow easily. (p. 295)

invertebrate (in vûr′tə brit′) An animal without a backbone. (p. 214)

involuntary muscle (in vol′ən ter′ē mus′əl) A muscle that causes movements you cannot control. (p. 449)

irrigation (ir′i gā′shən) A way to get water into the soil by artificial means. (p. 422)

J

joint (joint) A place where two or more bones meet. (p. 438)

K

kidney (kid′nē) One of two main waste-removal organs in vertebrates that filters wastes from the blood. (p. 254)

kilogram (kil′ə gram′) The metric unit used to measure mass. (p. 70)

kingdom (king′dəm) One of the largest groups of organisms into which an organism can be classified. (p. 28)

L

larva (lär′və) A wormlike stage of some organisms that hatches from an egg during complete metamorphosis; a young organism with a form different from its parents. (p. 266)

lava (lä′və) Magma that reaches Earth's surface through volcanoes or cracks. (p. 151)

learned behavior (lûrnd bi hāv′yər) Behavior that is not inborn. (p. 281)

length (lengkth) The number of units that fit along one edge of something. (p. 80)

lever (lev′ər) A simple machine made of a rigid bar on a pivot point. (p. 132)

life cycle (līf sī′kəl) The stages of growth and change of an organism's life. (p. 266)

life span (līf span) How long an organism can be expected to live. (p. 267)

ligament (lig′ə mənt) A tough band of tissue that holds two bones together where they meet. (p. 439)

lightning (līt′ ning) A discharge of static electricity from a cloud to another cloud or to the ground. (p. 296)

liquid (lik′wid) A form of matter that takes up a definite amount of space and has no definite shape. (p. 71)

load (lōd) The object being lifted or moved. (p. 132)

LSD (el es dē) A mind-altering drug. (p. 473)

luster (lus′tər) The way a mineral reflects light. (p. 149)

M

magma (mag′mə) Melted rock material. (p. 151)

magnetic field (mag net′ik fēld) A region of magnetic force around a magnet. (p. 332)

mammal (mam′əl) A warm-blooded vertebrate with hair or fur that feeds milk to its young; most are born live. (p. 242)

mantle (man′təl) The layer of rock lying below the crust. (p. 202)

marijuana (mar′ə wä′nə) An illegal drug made from the crushed leaves, flowers, and seeds of the cannabis plant. (p. 473)

marrow (mar′ō) Soft tissue that fills some bones. (p. 437)

mass (mas) The amount of matter making up an object. (p. 70)

mass extinction (mas ek stingk′shən) The dying out at the same time of many different species. (p. 44)

matter (ma′tər) Anything that takes up space and has properties that you can observe and describe. (p. 68)

melt (melt) When water particles absorb heat energy and change from a solid to a liquid. (p. 387)

metamorphic rock (met′ə môr′fik rok) Rock whose form has been changed by heat and/or pressure. (p. 154)

metamorphosis (met′ə môr′fə sis) A process of changes during certain animals′ development. (p. 264)

metric system (met′rik sis′təm) A system of measurement based on units of ten. (p. 80)

microorganism (mī′krō ôr′gə niz′əm) An organism that is so small you need a microscope to see it. (p. 8)

migrate (mī′grāt) An instinct that causes some animals to move to a different area to either avoid cold weather, find new food supplies, or find a safe place to breed and raise their young. (p. 280)

mimicry (mim′i krē) When one organism imitates the traits of another. (p. 278)

mineral (min′ər əl) A naturally occurring substance, neither plant nor animal. (p. 148)

misuse (v., mis ūz′) To use a legal drug improperly or in an unsafe way. (p. 474)

mixture (miks′chər) Two or more types of matter that are mixed together and keep their own properties. (p. 92)

mold (mōld) n., A fossil clearly showing the outside features of the organism. (p. 163)

mollusk (mol′əsk) A soft-bodied invertebrate. (p. 226)

molting (mōl′ting) A process by which an arthropod sheds its exoskeleton. (p. 228)

moraine (mə rān′) Rock debris carried and deposited as a glacier melts. (p. 177)

PRONUNCIATION KEY

a at; ā ape; ä far; âr care; e end; ē me; i it; ī ice; îr pierce; o hot; ō old; ô fork; oi oil; ou out; u up; ū use; ü rule; u̇ pull; ûr turn; hw white; ng song; th thin; th this; zh measure; ə about, taken, pencil, lemon, circus

movable joint (mü′və bəl joint) A place where bones meet and can move easily. (p. 438)

movable pulley (mü′və bəl pùl′ē) A pulley that increases the effort force needed to move an object. The pulley wheel can change position, but the direction of the force remains unchanged. *See* **pulley**. (p. 134)

muscular system (mus′kyə lər sis′təm) The organ system made up of muscles that move bones. (pp. 256, 449)

N

narcotic (när kot′ik) A type of medicine that is used as a painkiller. (p. 473)

nervous system (nûr′vəs sis′təm) The organ system that controls all other body systems. (p. 257)

newton (nü′tən) A metric unit for weight, measuring the amount of pull or push a force such as gravity produces between two masses. (p. 83)

nicotine (nik′ə tēn′) A poisonous, oily substance found in tobacco. (p. 462)

nucleus (nü′klē əs) A cell's central control station. (p. 15)

nymph (nimf) A stage of some organisms that hatch from an egg during incomplete metamorphosis; a nymph is a young insect that looks like an adult. (p. 267)

O

omnivore (om′ nə vôr′) A consumer that eats both animals and plants (p. 56)

open circuit (ō′pən sûr′kit) A broken or incomplete path that electricity cannot flow through. (p. 305)

order (ôr′dər) A smaller group within a class. Orders are made up of still smaller groups of similar organisms called *families*. (p. 30)

organ (ôr′gən) A group of tissues that work together to do a certain job. (p. 6)

organ system (ôr′gən sis′təm) A group of organs that work together to carry on life functions. (p. 6)

organism (ôr′gə niz′əm) A living thing that carries out five basic life functions on its own. (p. 4)

outer core (ou′tər kôr) A liquid layer of Earth lying below the mantle. (p. 202)

outwash plain (out′wôsh plān) Gravel, sand, and clay carried from glaciers by melting water and streams. (p. 179)

over-the-counter (ō′vər thə koun′tər) Said of a medicine that can be purchased off the shelves in stores. (p. 470)

oxygen (ok′sə jən) A part of the air that is needed by most organisms to live. (p. 4)

P

parallel circuit (par′ə lel′ sûr′kit) A circuit in which each energy-using device is connected to the cell separately. (p. 317)

partly immovable joint (pärt′lē i mü′və bəl joint) A place where bones meet and can move only a little. (p. 438)

passive smoke (pas′iv smōk) Smoke that is inhaled by someone other than the smoker. (p. 463)

penicillin (pen′ə sil′in) A type of antibiotic first developed from a type of mold. (p. 470)

periodic (pîr′ē od′ik) Repeating in a pattern, like the *periodic* table of the elements. (p. 90)

permeability (pûr′mē ə bil′i tē) The rate at which water can pass through a material. Water passes quickly through porous soils with a high permeability. (p. 191)

pesticide (pes′tə sīd′) A chemical that kills insects. (p. 423)

petrified (pet′rə fīd′) Said of parts of plants or animals, especially wood and bone, that have been preserved by being "turned to stone." (p. 165)

pharmacist (fär′mə sist) A person trained and licensed to prepare and give out medicines according to a doctor's orders. (p. 470)

phylum (fī′ləm), *pl.* **phyla** (fī′lə) A smaller group into which members of a kingdom are further classified. Members share at least one major characteristic, like having a backbone. (pp. 30, 222)

physical change (fiz′i kəl chānj) A change that begins and ends with the same type of matter. *See* **chemical change**. (p. 107)

plasma (plaz′mə) The liquid part of blood. (p. 252)

pole (pōl) One of two ends of a magnet; where a magnet's pull is strongest. (p. 330)

population (pop′yə lā′shən) One type of organism living in an area. (p. 50)

pore space (pôr spās) Any of the gaps between soil particles, usually filled with water and air. *Porous* soils have large, well-connected pore spaces. (pp. 190, 408)

precipitation (pri sip′i tā′shən) Water in the atmosphere that falls to Earth as rain, snow, hail, or sleet. (p. 386)

prescription (pri skrip′shən) An order from a doctor, usually for medicine. (p. 470)

producer (prə dü′sər) An organism, such as a plant, that makes food. (p. 54)

property (prop′ər tē) A characteristic of something that you can observe, such as mass, volume, weight, and density. (p. 68)

protective resemblance (prə tek′tiv ri zem′bləns) A type of adaptation in which an animal resembles something in its environment. (p. 276)

protist (prō′tist) Any of a variety of one-celled organisms that live in pond water. (p. 19)

pulley (pùl′ē) A grooved wheel that turns by the action of a rope in the groove. *See* **fixed pulley** and **movable pulley**. (p. 134)

pupa (pū′pə) A stage of some organisms that follows the larva stage in complete metamorphosis; many changes take place as adult tissues and organs form. (p. 266)

R

radial symmetry (rā′dē əl sim′ə trē) A form of symmetry in which an animal has matching body parts that extend outward from a central point. (p. 215)

radiate (rā′dē āt′) To send energy traveling in all directions through space. (p. 354)

radiation (rā′dē ā′shən) The transfer of heat through space. (p. 119)

rechargeable battery (rē charj′ə bəl bat′ə rē) A battery in which the chemical reactions can be reversed by a recharger, allowing these batteries to be used again and again. (p. 357)

reflex (rē′fleks′) The simplest inherited behavior, which is automatic, like an animal scratching an itch. (p. 280)

regeneration (rē jen′ə rā′shən) A form of asexual reproduction in simple animals in which a whole animal develops from just a part of the original animal. (p. 268)

relative age (rel′ə tiv āj) The age of something compared to the age of another thing. (p. 153)

PRONUNCIATION KEY

a at; ā ape; ä far; âr care; e end; ē me; i it; ī ice; îr pierce; o hot; ō old; ô fork; oi oil; ou out; u up; ū use; ü rule; ù pull; ûr turn; hw white; ng song; th thin; <u>th</u> this; zh measure; ə about, taken, pencil, lemon, circus

GLOSSARY

reptile (rep'təl) A cold-blooded vertebrate that lives on land and has a backbone, an endoskeleton, and waterproof skin with scales or plates. (p. 240)

resistor (ri zis'tər) A material through which electricity has difficulty flowing. (p. 307)

respiratory system (res'pər ə tôr'ē sis'təm) The organ system that brings oxygen to body cells and removes waste gas. (p. 253)

rock cycle (rok sī'kəl) A never-ending process by which rocks are changed from one type to another. (p. 155)

rock debris (rok də brē') Boulders, rock fragments, gravel, sand, and soil that are picked up by a glacier as it moves. (p. 176)

runoff (run'ôf') The water that flows over Earth's surface but does not evaporate or soak into the ground. (p. 409)

S

scale (skāl) An instrument used to measure weight. (p. 83)

screw (skrü) An inclined plane that is wrapped around a pole. (p. 137)

sediment (sed'ə mənt) Deposited rock particles and other materials that settle in a liquid. (p. 152)

sedimentary rock (sed'ə men'tə rē rok) Rock formed from bits or layers of rocks cemented together. (p. 152)

seismic wave (sīz'mik wāv) A vibration caused by rocks moving and breaking along faults. (p. 200)

seismogram (sīz'mə gram') The record of seismic waves made by a seismograph. (p. 201)

seismograph (sīz'mə graf') An instrument that detects, measures, and records the energy of earthquake vibrations. (p. 198)

septic tank (sep'tik tangk) An underground tank in which sewage is broken down by bacteria. (p. 425)

series circuit (sîr'ēz sûr'kit) A circuit in which the current must flow through one energy-using device in order to flow through the other. (p. 316)

sewage (sü'ij) Water mixed with waste. (p. 425)

sewer (sü'ər) A large pipe or channel that carries sewage to a sewage treatment plant. (p. 425)

sexual reproduction (sek'shü əl rē'prə duk'shən) Producing offspring with two parents. (p. 268)

short circuit (shôrt sûr'kit) When too much current flows through a conductor. (p. 308)

side effect (sīd i fekt') An unwanted result of using a medicine. (p. 471)

simple machine (sim'pəl mə shēn') A machine with few moving parts that makes it easier to do work. (p. 130)

skeletal muscle (skel'i təl mus'əl) A muscle that is attached to a bone and allows movement. (p. 446)

skeletal system (skel'i təl sis'təm) The organ system made up of bones, cartilage, and ligaments. (pp. 256, 439)

skeleton (skel'i tən) An internal supporting frame that gives the body its shape and protects many organs. (p. 436)

smooth muscle (smüth mus'əl) The type of muscle that makes up internal organs and blood vessels. (p. 449)

soil profile (soil prō'fil) A vertical section of soil from the surface down to bedrock. (p. 187)

soil water (soil wô'tər) Water that soaks into the ground. (p. 374)

solid (sol'id) A form of matter that has a definite shape and takes up a definite amount of space. (p. 70)

species (spē'shēz) The smallest classification group, made up of only one type of organism that can reproduce with others of the same species; for example, all dogs belong to the same species. (p. 30)

sperm (spûrm) The male sex cell. (p. 269)

spherical symmetry (sfer'i kəl sim'ə trē) A form of symmetry in which the parts of an animal with a round body match up when it is folded through its center. (p. 215)

sponge (spunj) The simplest kind of invertebrate. (p. 214)

sprain (sprān) A pull or tear in a muscle or ligament. (p. 439)

standard unit (stan'dərd ū'nit) A unit of measure that people all understand and agree to use. (p. 80)

state (stāt) A form of matter, such as a solid, liquid, or gas; how quickly the particles of matter vibrate, how much heat energy they have, and how they are arranged determine the state of matter. (p. 70)

static electricity (stat'ik i lek tris'i tē) A buildup of an electrical charge. (p. 294)

stimulant (stim'yə lənt) A substance that speeds up the activity of the body. (p. 462)

streak plate (strēk plāt) A glass plate that a mineral can be rubbed against to find out the color of the streak it leaves. (p. 149)

subsoil (sub'soil') A hard layer of clay and minerals that lies beneath topsoil. (p. 187)

surface current (sûr'fis kûr'ənt) The movement of the ocean caused by steady winds blowing over the ocean. (p. 397)

switch (swich) A device that can open or close an electric circuit. (p. 309)

symmetry (sim'ə trē) The way an animal's body parts match up around a point or central line. (p. 214)

system (sis'təm) A group of parts that work together. (p. 6)

T

tar (tär) A sticky, brown substance found in tobacco. (p. 462)

temperature (tem'pər ə chər) A measure of how hot or cold something is. (p. 121)

tendon (ten'dən) A strong band of tissue that connects a muscle to bone. (p. 447)

terminal (tûr'mə nəl) One of two places where wires can be attached to a cell or battery. (p. 306)

terminus (tûr'mə nəs) The end, or outer margin, of a glacier where rock debris accumulates. (p. 177)

thermometer (thər mom'i tər) An instrument used to measure temperature. (p. 121)

tide (tīd) The rise and fall of ocean water levels. (p. 398)

tissue (tish'ü) A group of similar cells that work together to carry out a job. (p. 5)

topsoil (top'soil') The dark, top layer of soil, rich in humus and minerals, in which many tiny organisms live and most plants grow. (p. 187)

trait (trāt) A characteristic of an organism. (p. 28)

tranquilizer (trang'kwə lī'zər) A type of medicine used to calm a person. (p. 472)

PRONUNCIATION KEY

a **at**; ā **ape**; ä **far**; âr **care**; e **end**; ē **me**; i **it**; ī **ice**; îr **pierce**; o **hot**; ō **old**; ô **fork**; oi **oil**; ou **out**; u **up**; ū **use**; ü **rule**; u **pull**; ûr **turn**; hw **white**; ng **song**; th **thin**; <u>th</u> **this**; zh **measure**; ə **about, taken, pencil, lemon, circus**

transformer (trans fôr'mər) A device in which alternating current in one coil produces current in a second coil. (p. 346)

transpiration (tran'spə rā'shən) The process whereby plants release water vapor into the air through their leaves. (p. 411)

triceps (trī'seps) A muscle on the outside of the upper arm that straightens the arm by contracting. (p. 446)

U

urine (yür'in) The concentrated wastes filtered by the kidneys. (p. 254)

V

vacuole (vak'ū ōl') A holding bin for food, water, and waste. (p. 15)

vertebrate (vûr'tə brāt') An animal with a backbone. (p. 214)

virus (vī'rəs) Nonliving particles smaller than cells that are able to reproduce inside living cells. (p. 20)

volt (vōlt) A unit for measuring the force that makes negative charges flow. (p. 345)

volume (vol'ūm) How much space an object takes up. (p. 81)

voluntary muscle (vol'ən ter'ē mus'əl) A muscle that causes movements you can control. (p. 449)

W

warm-blooded (wôrm'blud'id) Said of an animal with a constant body temperature. (p. 236)

water conservation (wôtər kon'sər vā'shən) The use of water-saving methods. (p. 426)

water cycle (wô'tər sī'kəl) The continuous movement of water between Earth's surface and the air, changing from liquid to gas to liquid. (p. 388)

water table (wô'tər tā'bəl) The upper area of groundwater. (p. 408)

water treatment plant (wô'tər trēt'mənt plant) A place where water is made clean and pure. (p. 424)

water vapor (wô'tər vā'pər) Water as a gas in Earth's atmosphere. (p. 372)

wave (wāv) An up-and-down movement of water. (p. 399)

weathering (weth'ər ing) The process of breaking down rocks into smaller pieces that create sediment. (p. 155)

wedge (wej) A simple machine made by combining two inclined planes. It translates a downward force into two outward forces in opposite directions. (p. 137)

weight (wāt) The measure of the pull of gravity between an object and Earth. (p. 83)

wet cell (wet sel) A device that produces electricity using two different metal bars placed in an acid solution. (p. 344)

wheel and axle (hwēl and ak'səl) A simple machine made of a handle or axis attached to the center of a wheel. (p. 135)

work (wûrk) To apply a force that makes an object move. An object must move some distance to call what happens work. (p. 128)

INDEX

*Indicates an activity related to this topic.

INDEX

INDEX

*Indicates an activity related to this topic.

INDEX

W

*Indicates an activity related to this topic.

CREDITS

Design & Production: Kirchoff/Wohlberg, Inc.

Maps: Geosystems.

Transvision: Stephen Ogilvy (photography); Guy Porfirio (illustration).

Illustrations: Kenneth Batelman: pp. 74, 105, 121; Dan Brown: pp. 376, 384, 385, 388-389, 389, 398, 399, 400, 408, 410; Elizabeth Callen: pp. 284, 368; Barbara Cousins: pp. 252, 253, 254, 255, 256, 257, 266; Steven Cowden: pp. 296, 297, 298, 318-319, 348, 354; Michael DiGiorgio: pp. 56, 58, 215, 222, 236; Jeff Fagan: pp. 132, 133, 137; Howard S. Friedman: p. 54; Colin Hayes: pp. 127, 134, 135, 310, 333, 343, 346, 347, 445, R7, R11, R13, R15, R20-R23; Tom Leonard: pp. 4, 5, 6, 16, 42, 43, 44, 51, 213, 225, 237, 264, 265, 268, 271, 332, 335, 344, 356, 362, 370, 436, 437, 438, 446, 447, 448, 449, 459; Olivia: pp. 24, 61, 64, 100, 141, 172, 205, 248, 285, 294, 326, 365, 404, 429, 454, 477, R2-R4, R9, R10, R13, R16-R19, R23-R25; Sharron O'Neil: pp. 14, 15, 20, 28, 31, 40, 41, 153, 176, 186, 190, 191, 374, 411; Vilma Ortiz-Dillon: pp. 144, 208, 386, 396, 397, 421, 424, 425, 432; Rob Schuster: pp. 84, 108, 117, 118, 120, 179, 307, 322, 342, 355, 358, 359; Matt Straub: pp. 7, 33, 243, 458, 461, 480; Ted Williams: pp. 69, 92, 93, 95, 119, 154, 155, 198, 200, 201, 202, 338-339, 392-393, 456, 457, 463, 465, 469; Craig Zolman: pp. 303, 304, 305, 306, 308, 309, 316, 317, 318, 319, 320, 321, 368.

Photography Credits:

Contents: iii: Jim Battles/Debinsky Photo Associates. iv: inset, Corbis; Richard Price/FPG. v: E.R. Degginger/Bruce Coleman, Inc. vi: R. Williams/Bruce Coleman, Inc. vii: Jim Foster/The Stock Market. viii: Steve Wilkings/The Stock Market. ix: Mehau Kulyk/Science Photo Library.

National Geographic Invitation to Science: S2: t. Michael Nichols/National Geographic; b. Vanne Goodall. S3: t., b. Michael Nichols/National Geographic.

Be a Scientist: S4: bkgrd. Paul S. Howell/Liaison Agency; inset, Stuart Westmorland/Tony Stone Images. S5: David Mager. S6: t. Steven M. Barnett; m. The Granger Collection, New York; b. Corbis. S7: t. Bruce Avera Hunter/National Geographic Society-Image Collection; b. Michael Justice/Liaison. S8: Eric Neurath/Stock, Boston. S10: Robert Halstead-TPI/Masterfile. S11: l. Stuart Westmorland/Tony Stone Images; r. Steinhart Aquarium/Tom McHugh/Photo Researchers, Inc. S12: James Stanfield. S13: l. Tom Tracy/Tony Stone Images; c. Steven M. Barnett; r. Andrew Wood/Photo Researchers, Inc. S14: The Granger Collection, New York. S15: t. National Geographic Society Photographic Laboratory; b. David Mager. S16: t., b. David Doubilet. S17: Jeff Rotman/Tony Stone Images. S19: Stephen Ogilvy.

Unit 1: 1: F.C. Millington/TCL Masterfile; John Lythgoe/TCL Masterfile. 2: Stephen Ogilvy. 3: t., b. Stephen Ogilvy. 7: Stephen Ogilvy. 8: l. David M. Philipps/Photo Researchers, Inc.; r. Astrid & Hanns-Frieder/Photo Researchers, Inc.; b.l. Michael Abbey/Photo Researchers, Inc; b.r. Edward R. Degginger/Bruce Coleman, Inc. 9: Ann & Carl Purcell/Words & Pictures/PNI. 10: l. Enrico Ferorelli; r. Phyllis Picardi/Stock, Boston/PNI. 11: Dan McCoy/Rainbow/PNI. 12: Stephen Ogilvy. 13: Nigel Cattlin/Photo Researchers, Inc. 17: Stephen Ogilvy. 18: l. & r. PhotoDisc; inset t.l. & inset t.r. Biophoto Associates/Photo Researchers, Inc.; inset b.l. Ken Edward/Photo Researchers, Inc.; inset b.r. J.F. Gennaro/Photo Researchers, Inc. 19: t.l. M.I. Walker/Photo Researchers, Inc.; m.l. Biophoto Associates/Photo Researchers, Inc.; b.l. Eric V. Grave/Photo Researchers, Inc.; inset r. CNRI/Science Photo/Photo Researchers, Inc.; r. Joy Spur/Bruce Coleman, Inc. 21: Doctor Dennis Kunkel/Phototake/PNI. 22-23: David Scharf/Peter Arnold, Inc. 23: R. Maisonneuvre/Photo Researchers, Inc.; V.I. LAB E.R.I.C./FPG. 25: Tom & Pat Leeson. 26: Stephen Ogilvy. 27: t.l. Gregory Ochocki/Photo Researchers, Inc.; t.r. J. Foott/Tom Stack & Associates; m.l. Kjell B. Sandved; m.r. Charlie Heidecker/Visuals Unlimited; m.l. Carl R. Sams II/Peter Arnold, Inc.; m.r. Richard Schiell/Animals Animals; b.l. Hans Pfletschinger/Peter Arnold, Inc.; b.r. Mike Bacon/Tom Stack & Associates. 29: M.I. Walker/Photo Researchers, Inc. 30: Margaret Miller/Photo Researchers, Inc. 32: Stephen Ogilvy. 33: PhotoDisc. 34: l. Richard R. Hansen/Photo Researchers, Inc.; r. Jany Sauvanet/Photo Researchers, Inc.; b. Kevin Schafer/Corbis. 35: l. Adam Jones/Photo Researchers, Inc.; m. Stephen Dalton/Photo Researchers, Inc.; r. Scott Camazine/Photo Researchers, Inc. 36: Dieter & Mary Plage/Bruce Coleman, Inc. 37: Edward R. Degginger/Bruce Coleman, Inc. 38: Francois Gohier/Photo Researchers, Inc. 39: l. Biophoto Associates/Photo Researchers, Inc.; r. Edward R. Degginger/Photo Researchers, Inc. 41: Stephen Ogilvy. 43: Charles E. Mohr/Photo Researchers, Inc. 45: Tom McHugh/Photo Researchers, Inc. 46: Project Lokahi. 46-47: Ken Lucas/Visuals Unlimited. 48: Stephen J. Krasemann/Photo Researchers, Inc. 49: Stephen Ogilvy. 50: Stephen Ogilvy. 51: Stephen Ogilvy. 52: l. Stephen Krasemann/Photo Researchers, Inc.; m. Jim Steinberg/Photo Researchers, Inc.; r. Renee Lynn/Photo Researchers, Inc. 53: b.l. C.K. Lorenz/Photo Researchers, Inc.; m. Leonide Principe/Photo Researchers, Inc.; r. F. Stuart Westmorland/Photo Researchers, Inc. 55: t. Microfield Scientific/Photo Researchers, Inc.; b. Andrew J. Martinez/Photo Researchers, Inc. 56: inset, Charlie Ott/Photo Researchers, Inc. 56-57: Stephen Dalton/Photo Researchers, Inc. 57: r. Stephen Ogilvy. 59: Arthur Tilley/FPG. 60: Chinch Gryniewicz/Ecoscene/Corbis.

Unit 2: 65: Picture Perfect; Phil Degginger/Bruce Coleman, Inc. 66: PhotoDisc. 67: Stephen Ogilvy. 68: Stephen Ogilvy. 70: Stephen Ogilvy. 71: r. PhotoDisc; l. Stephen Ogilvy. 72: r. Charles Gupton/AllStock/PNI; l. Stephen Ogilvy. 73: all Stephen Ogilvy. 74: Stephen Ogilvy. 75: Stephen Ogilvy. 76: l. James A. Sugar/Black Star/PNI; r. Lisa Quinones/Black Star/PNI. 77: James A. Sugar/Black Star/PNI. 78: Stephen Ogilvy. 79: Stephen Ogilvy. 80: PhotoDisc. 82: Stephen Ogilvy. 83: Stephen Ogilvy. 84: Stephen Ogilvy. 85: Craig Tuttle/The Stock Market. 86: Stephen Ogilvy. 87: t. BIPM; b. Stockbyte. 88: PhotoDisc. 89: Stephen Ogilvy. 91: Corbis/Bettmann. 92: Stephen Ogilvy. 94: Stephen Ogilvy. 95: Stephen Ogilvy. 96: PhotoDisc; (soda can) Steven Needham/Envision. 97: Stephen Ogilvy. 98: t. Science Photo Library/Photo Researchers, Inc. 98-99: b. Chris Collins/The Stock Market. 99: Corbis/Bettmann. 101: Stock Imagery, Inc.; E.J. West/Stock Imagery, Inc. 102: l. Jean Higgins/Envision; r. Rafael Macia/Photo Researchers, Inc. 103: Stephen Ogilvy. 104: col 1: l. Michael Keller/FPG; r. Charles Winters/Photo Researchers, Inc.; col 2: t. Ron Rovtar/FPG; b. James L. Amos/Photo Researchers, Inc. 106: l. Stephen Ogilvy; r.t. R.B. Smith/Dembinsky Photo; r.b. Charles Winters/Photo Researchers, Inc. 109: Stephen Ogilvy. 110: col 1: t. Gerald Zanetti/The Stock Market; m. Biophoto Associates/Photo Researchers, Inc.; b. Philip James Corwin/Corbis; col 2: t. Robert Jonathan Kligge/The Stock Market; m. Brownie Harris/The Stock Market; b. Adam Hart-Davis/Photo Researchers, Inc.; 111: Stephen Ogilvy. 112: t. Joel Arrington/Visuals Unlimited; m. David McGlynn/FPG; b. Paul Bierman/Visuals Unlimited. 112-113: PhotoDisc. 113: Sylvan Wittwer/Visuals Unlimited. 114: Richard Ellis/Photo Researchers, Inc. 115: Stephen Ogilvy. 116: Stephen Ogilvy. 117: Stephen Ogilvy. 119: Stephen Ogilvy. 122: t. Edward R. Degginger/Bruce Coleman, Inc.; m. Tim Davis/Photo Researchers, Inc.; b. Hans Reinhard/Bruce Coleman, Inc. 124: PhotoDisc; Ken Karp. 125: Jade Albert/FPG. 126: Debra P. Hershkowitz. 128: l. Idaho Ketchum/The Stock Market; r. Dollarhide Monkmeyer. 129: Hank Morgan/Photo Researchers, Inc. 130: l. Steve Elmore/Bruce Coleman, Inc.; b. Edward R. Degginger/Bruce Coleman, Inc.; r. J. Fennell/Bruce Coleman, Inc. 131: l. Tony Freeman/PhotoEdit; c. Kenneth H. Thomas/Photo Researchers, Inc.; t.r. Tony Freeman/PhotoEdit; b.r. Science VU/Visuals Unlimited. 133: David Mager. 135: Alan Schein/The Stock Market. 136: David Young-Wolff/PhotoEdit. 138: Michal Newman/PhotoEdit. 139: PhotoDisc. 140: l. Culver Pictures, Inc.; m. www.artoday.com.

Unit 3: 145: Carr Clifton; Tom Bean. 146: Sinclair Stammers/Photo Researchers, Inc. 147: Stephen Ogilvy. 148: l.&m.r. Ken Karp; m.l. ©Tom Pantages/Photo Take; r. Stephen Ogilvy; b. Joyce Photographics/Photo Researchers, Inc. 149: t.r. Corbis; t.l. Stephen Ogilvy; b.r. A.J. Copley/VU; b.l. Mark A. Schneider/VU. 150: PhotoDisc. 151: l. Stephen Ogilvy; m.&r. E.R. Degginger/Photo Researchers, Inc. 152: t.l. Charles Winters/Photo Researchers, Inc.; t.r. Ken Karp; b.l. ©Martin G. Miller/VU; b.r. Andrew J. Martinez/Photo Researchers, Inc. 153: Stephen Ogilvy. 154: Corbis. 156: t. J C Carton/Bruce Coleman, Inc.; b. Edward R. Degginger/Bruce Coleman, Inc. 157: Stephen Ogilvy. 158: t. David Burnett/Contract Press Images/PNI; b. E.R. Degginger/Photo Researchers, Inc. 159: NASA. 160: l. Weststock; m. PhotoDisc. 162: Francois Gohier/Photo Researchers, Inc.; 163: l. Charles R. Belinky/Photo Researchers, Inc.; r. Stephen Ogilvy. 164: l. Edward R. Degginger/Bruce Coleman, Inc.; r. Novosti/Photo Researchers, Inc. 165: l. A.J. Copley/Visuals Unlimited; r. Ed Bohon/The Stock Market. 166: Carlos Goldin/Photo Researchers, Inc. 167: A.J. Copley/Visuals Unlimited. 168: l. Tom McHugh/Photo Researchers, Inc.; r. A.J. Copley/Visuals Unlimited. 169: l. Phototake/PNI; r. Phil Degginger/Bruce Coleman, Inc. 170: Richard Lydekker/Linda Hall Library. 171: courtesy Lisa White. 173: N.&M. Freeman/Bruce Coleman, Inc. 174: Lee Foster/Bruce Coleman, Inc. 175: Stephen Ogilvy. 177: Charlie

R47

Heidecker/Visuals Unlimited. 178: Ken Cavanagh. 180: John Serrao/ Photo Researchers, Inc. 181: Joyce Photographics/Photo Researchers, Inc. 182-183: Ron Sanford/The Stock Market. 183: Photo Researchers, Inc. 184: Stephen Ogilvy. 185: Stephen Ogilvy. 187: Black/Bruce Coleman, Inc. 188: Stephen Ogilvy. 188-189: Janis Burger/Bruce Coleman, Inc. 190: Stephen Ogilvy. 192: Kazuyoshi Nomachi/Photo Researchers, Inc. 193: Richard T. Nowitz/Photo Researchers, Inc. 195: t.r. Barry Hennings/Photo Researchers, Inc.; b.l. Franco Sal- Moiragni/The Stock Market; t.l. Gary S. Withey/Bruce Coleman, Inc.; bkgrd. Lynette Cook/Science Photo Library/Photo Researchers, Inc. 196: Stephen Ogilvy. 197: Stephen Ogilvy. 199: l. PhotoDisc; r. Stephen Ogilvy. 203: Russell D. Curtis/Photo Researchers, Inc. 204: Corbis.

Unit 4: 209: Art Wolf/Tony Stone Images. 210: Hans Reinhard/Bruce Coleman, Inc. 211: Stephen Ogilvy. 212: l. Maryann Frazier/Photo Researchers, Inc.; r. Scott Smith/Animals Animals. 214: l. Stephen Ogilvy; r. Charles V. Angelo/Photo Researchers, Inc. 216: t.r. Joe McDonald/Bruce Coleman, Inc.; m.r. James R. McCullagh/Visuals Unlimited; b.l. Neil S. McDaniel/Photo Researchers, Inc.; b.c. Ron & Valerie Taylor/Bruce Coleman, Inc.; b.r. John Chellman/Animals Animals. 217: l. David Doubilet; r. Andrew J. Martinez/Photo Researchers, Inc. 218: Sisse Brimberg/National Geographic Image Collection. 219: t. Fran Coleman/Animals Animals; b. Joel Sartore. 220: l. & r. Chip Clark. 221: t. Kim Taylor/Bruce Coleman, Inc; b. Ray Coleman/Photo Researchers, Inc. 223: inset, Marian Bacon/Animals Animals; t. Sefton/Bruce Coleman, Inc. 224: t. Carol Geake/Animals Animals; b. J.H. Robinson/ Photo Researchers, Inc. 226: l. Joyce & Frank Burek/Animals Animals; b.r. Zig Leszcynski/Animals Animals. 227: Doug Sokell/Visuals Unlimited. 228: l. Jane Burton/Bruce Coleman, Inc.; r. Tom McHugh/ Photo Researchers, Inc. 229: col 1: L. West/Photo Researchers, Inc.; insets l. & r. Dwight Kuhn; col 2 clockwise from top: L. West/Bruce Coleman, Inc.; John D. Cunningham/Visuals Unlimited; Mary Beth Angelo/Photo Researchers, Inc.; Cabisco/Visuals Unlimited; Fabio Colombini/Animals Animals; Mary Snyderman/Visuals Unlimited. 230- 231: L. Newman A./Photo Researchers, Inc. 231: William J. Pohley/ Visuals Unlimited. 232: t.l. Richard Hamilton Smith/Dembinsky Photo Assoc. 232-233: PhotoDisc. 233: t. Richard T. Nowitz/Photo Researchers,Inc.; David Young-Wolf/PhotoEdit. 234: Stephen Ogilvy. 235: Norman Owen Tomalin/Bruce Coleman, Inc. 237: Hans Reinhard/ Bruce Coleman, Inc. 238: Dave B. Fleetham/Visuals Unlimited; inset, Jane Burton/Bruce Coleman, Inc. 239: t. G.I. Bernard/OSF Animals Animals; b. L. West/Bruce Coleman, Inc. 240: Tom McHugh/Photo Researchers, Inc. 241: Roy David Farris/Visuals Unlimited. 242: Jean Phillipe Varin/Photo Researchers, Inc. 243: clockwise from t.l.: Dan Guravich/Photo Researchers, Inc.; Ron & Valerie Taylor/Bruce Coleman, Inc.; Jeff Lepore/Photo Researchers, Inc.; Dwight R. Kuhn; Wally Eberhart/Visuals Unlimited; Zig Leszcynski/Animals Animals. 244: Stephen Ogilvy. 245: t. Eric & David Hosking/Corbis; b. W. Perry Conway/Corbis. 246: Douglas Faulkner/Photo Researchers, Inc. 247: inset, Kennan Ward/Bruce Coleman, Inc.; bkgrd. Peter B. Kaplan/Photo Researchers, Inc. 249: Charles Krebs/Tony Stone Images; L.L. Rue III/Bruce Coleman, Inc. 250: PhotoDisc. 251: Stephen Ogilvy. 258: Kjell B. Sandved/Photo Researchers, Inc. 259: Stephen Spotte/Photo Researchers, Inc. 260: PhotoDisc. 261: b.r. PhotoDisc; t.l. Larry Cameron/Photo Researchers, Inc.; t.r. Norman Owen Tomalin/Bruce Coleman, Inc. 262: Gerard Lacz/Animals Animals. 263: Stephen Ogilvy. 270: Stephen Ogilvy. 271: AP/Wide World Photos. 272: Stephen Ogilvy. 273: b.r. D. Long/Visuals Unlimited; bkgrd. G. Buttner/Okapia/Photo Researchers, Inc.; r. Wally Eberhart/Visuals Unlimited. 274: Michael Fogden/Bruce Coleman, Inc. 276: Breck P. Kent/Animals Animals; Michael Fogden/Bruce Coleman, Inc. 277: K & K Ammann/Bruce Coleman, Inc. 278: John Shaw/Bruce Coleman, Inc. 280: l. Maria Zorn/Animals Animals; r. W.J.C. Murray/Bruce Coleman, Inc. 282: Rita Nannini/Photo Researchers, Inc. 283: A. Ramey/PhotoEdit. 284: PhotoDisc; b.r. Thomas C. Boyden/Dembinsky Photo Assoc.

Unit 5: 289: PhotoDisc. 290: Tim Davis/Photo Researchers, Inc. 291: Stephen Ogilvy. 292: Stockbyte. 293: PhotoDisc. 294: PhotoDisc. 295: Stephen Ogilvy. 297: Kent Wood/Photo Researchers, Inc. 299: PhotoDisc. 300: l. The Granger Collection, New York; r. Dale Camera Graphics/Phototake/PNI. 301: The Granger Collection, New York. 302: Stephen Ogilvy. 305: Stephen Ogilvy. 308: Stephen Ogilvy. 309: Norbert Wu. 311: Stephen Ogilvy. 312: b.l. Culver Pictures, Inc.; m. Stock Montage, Inc.; b.r. PhotoDisc; t.r. Rich Treptow/Photo Researchers, Inc. 313: m. Norman Owen Tomalin/Bruce Coleman, Inc.; b.r. Will & Deni McIntyre/Photo Researchers, Inc. 314: PhotoDisc. 315: Stephen Ogilvy. 322: l. PhotoDisc; r. Norman Owen Tomalin/Bruce Coleman, Inc. 323: Stephen Ogilvy. 324: Don Mason/The Stock Market. 324-325: Michael W. Davidson/Photo Researchers, Inc. 325: David Parker/Seagate/Photo Researchers, Inc. 327: PhotoDisc. 328: Stephen Ogilvy. 329: Stephen Ogilvy. 330: Stephen Ogilvy. 331: Stephen Ogilvy. 332: Stephen Ogilvy.

334: l. Stephen Ogilvy; r. David R. Frazier/Photo Researchers, Inc. 336: l. Stephen Ogilvy; r. Science Photo Library/Photo Researchers, Inc. 337: Stephen Ogilvy. 340: AP/Wide World Photos. 341: Stephen Ogilvy. 345: Stephen Ogilvy. 346: Ken Sherman/Bruce Coleman, Inc. 349: Historical Picture Archive/Corbis. 350: Stephen Ogilvy. 351: t. Elena Rooraid/PhotoEdit; b. Dennis Hallinan/FPG. 352: Stephen Ogilvy. 353: Stephen Ogilvy. 355: Stephen Ogilvy. 357: Stephen Ogilvy. 358: Stephen Ogilvy. 359: Stephen Ogilvy. 360: l. Martin Withers/Dembinsky Photo & PhotoDisc; c. Gelfan/Monkmeyer; r. Andrew/Photo Researchers, Inc. 360-361: PhotoDisc. 361: l. Charles D. Winters/Photo Researchers, Inc.; b. Stockbyte; r. Aaron Haupt/Photo Researchers, Inc. 363: Stephen Ogilvy. 364: bkgrd. Arthur Tilley/FPG; b.l. Robert Pettit/Dembinsky Photo; t.r. Schneider Studio/The Stock Market; b.r. Simon Fraser/Photo Researchers, Inc.; t.l. Werner Bertsch/Bruce Coleman, Inc.

Unit 6: 369: Picture Perfect; John Turner/Tony Stone Images. 371: Stephen Ogilvy. 372: Planet Earth Pictures/FPG. 373: l. PhotoDisc; r. Courtesy of Lake Michigan. 374: Roy Morsch/The Stock Market. 375: Joe McDonald/Bruce Coleman, Inc.; inset, Ron & Valerie Taylor. 377: Stephen Ogilvy. 378: Stephen Ogilvy. 379: Wendell Metzen/Bruce Coleman, Inc. 380-381: L.A. Frank, The University of Iowa & NASA/ Goddard Space Flight Center; Michael Freeman/Bruce Coleman, Inc./PNI; Chad Ehlers/Photo Network/PNI. 382: Stephen Ogilvy. 383: Stephen Ogilvy. 386: Stephen Ogilvy. 387: inset, Joe DiMaggio/The Stock Market; Lee Rentz/Bruce Coleman, Inc. 390: t. John Shaw/Bruce Coleman, Inc.; b. Howard B. Bluestein/Photo Researchers, Inc. 391: Steve Smith/FPG. 392: Library of Congress/Corbis. 393: l. Barry L. Runk/Grant Heilman; r. Charles D. Winters/Photo Researchers, Inc. 394: Stephen Ogilvy. 395: Stephen Ogilvy. 398: t. & b. Andrew J. Martinez/Photo Researchers, Inc. 399: Stephen Ogilvy. 401: bkgrd. & inset, Courtesy of Bruce M. Richmond/USGS. 402: Wendell Metzen/Bruce Coleman, Inc. 403: bkgrd. PhotoDisc; b. Gary Randall/ FPG; m. Martin Bond/Science Photo Library/Photo Researchers, Inc. 405: Superstock; Chris Vincent/The Stock Market. 406: Culver Pictures, Inc. 407: Stephen Ogilvy. 409: l. Michael S. Renner/Bruce Coleman, Inc.; r. Stephen Ogilvy. 412: l. PhotoDisc; inset, J. Dermid/Bruce Coleman, Inc. 413: Richard & Susan Day/Animals Animals. 414: Stephen Ogilvy. 415: PhotoDisc. 416: l. Corbis/Bettmann; r. AP/Wide World Photos. 416-417: Black/Bruce Coleman, Inc. 417: t.l. AP/Wide World Photos; t.r. Corbis/UPI/Bettman; b. AP/Wide World Photos. 418: PhotoDisc. 419: Stephen Ogilvy. 420: PhotoDisc. 421: Richard Hutchings/Photo Researchers, Inc. 422: all PhotoDisc. 423: b. PhotoDisc; r. Blackstone R. Millbury/Bruce Coleman, Inc. 425: Norman Owen Tomalin/Bruce Coleman, Inc. 426: John Elk III/Bruce Coleman, Inc. 427: Stephen Ogilvy. 428: m. David L. Pearson/Visuals Unlimited; bkgrd. John Shaw/Bruce Coleman; t. John Gerlach/Dembinsky Photo Assoc.

Unit 7: 433: Ken Chernus/FPG; J.Y. Mallet/PhotoEdit. 434: Adam Jones/ Dembinsky Photo. 435: Stephen Ogilvy. 439: Stephen Ogilvy. 441: Stephen Ogilvy. 442: l. Billy E. Barnes/PhotoEdit/PNI; r. Dept. of Clinical Radiology, Salisbury District Hospital/SPL/Photo Researchers, Inc. 444: Michael Krasowitz/FPG. 446: Dwight R. Kuhn. 447: l. & c. Stephen Ogilvy; r. Rob Curtis/VIREO. 448: CNRI/Photo Researchers, Inc. 449: Marshall Sklar/Photo Researchers, Inc. 450: Stephen Ogilvy. 451: Stephen Ogilvy. 452: b. Corbis; t. Mark E. Gibson/Dembinsky Photo. 453: t. Blair Seitz/Photo Researchers, Inc.; b. Mark Gibson/Visuals Unlimited. 455: Bill Losh/FPG. 458: Michael A. Keller/The Stock Market. 460: Stephen Ogilvy. 462: Matt Meadows/Peter Arnold, Inc. 463: Arthur Tilley/FPG. 466: PhotoDisc. 467: Mark C. Burnett/ Photo Researchers, Inc. 468: Stephen Ogilvy. 470: José Pelaez/The Stock Market. 473: Bill Beatty/Visuals Unlimited. 474: l. Stephen Ogilvy; r. Jeff Greenberg/PhotoEdit. 476: m. Barros & Barros/The Image Bank; t. Bill Bachmann/Photo Researchers, Inc.; bkgrd. Ed Gallucci/The Stock Market.

Handbook: Steven Ogilvy: pp. R6, R8, R12, R14, R15, R26.